DIVORCE
In New Jersey

A Self-Help Guide

Written and Published by Legal Services of New Jersey

Legal Education Handbook Series
LSNJ
...justice for all

ISBN 978-0-9790882-0-9

Table of Contents

Preface

Legal Services of New Jersey (LSNJ) coordinates the statewide Legal Services system in New Jersey, providing free legal assistance to low-income people in civil matters. Part of Legal Services' mission is to make people more aware of their legal rights and provide helpful information if they choose to pursue a legal case on their own. Awareness may allow you to resolve some problems on your own, without the need for a lawyer, or to make better use of a lawyer if you have one.

A Word of Caution About Using This Manual

This manual gives you general information about representing yourself in a divorce. This manual is written as if you are the spouse seeking the divorce. However, it also explains how to respond if your spouse has sued you for divorce. It contains forms and explains how to file for divorce in New Jersey based on separation, desertion, or extreme cruelty. The information, forms, and instructions in this manual are accurate as of May 2007. Before you take any of the steps outlined in this manual, you may want to speak to a lawyer to find out whether the law has changed since this manual was printed. You also should call the court to make sure addresses, fees, and court costs have not changed.

Important Information About Doing Your Own Divorce

This manual cannot provide specific advice about your divorce. It is not a substitute for having an attorney. Only a lawyer can give you specific advice about your case and help you protect all of your rights. Getting a divorce in New Jersey can be a complicated process. In the situations listed under *Getting Legal Advice* on page 2, it may be best to have a lawyer represent you in your divorce.

If you have questions about the court or are having problems getting information from court staff, you may contact the court ombudsman. Each local county courthouse has an ombudsman assigned to the job of explaining court procedures, programs, and services; helping self-represented litigants; making referrals to social services or other local agencies; and resolving complaints. The ombudsman may not give you legal advice, but he or she may provide contact information to lawyer referral services and Legal Services in each county. See Appendix E on page 118 for a list of names and phone numbers of each county court ombudsman.

If you are receiving public benefits, we recommend that you call LSNJ-LAW™, LSNJ's statewide, toll-free legal hotline, at 1-888-LSNJ-LAW (1-888-576-5529) for advice about how a divorce might affect your benefits. Hotline hours are Monday through Friday, 8 a.m. to 5:30 p.m. The term *public benefits* refers to financial assistance that some low-income families or individuals may be eligible to receive from local, county, or federal government. Public benefits include the different forms of welfare such as Temporary Assistance for Needy Families (TANF), General Assistance (GA), and Emergency Assistance (EA). Other benefits include food stamps (FS), Medicaid, and Supplemental Security Income (SSI). These programs all have limits on the amount of income a person can have in order to qualify for the benefits. If the income of a public benefits recipient increases, that recipient has a duty to report the increase to the public agency that provides the benefit. Failure to do this can result in sanctions or fines. For that reason, if you are receiving such benefits, you may want to consider asking an attorney about the effects of a divorce and property settlement on your continued eligibility for those benefits.

Getting Legal Advice

If you fit into any of the situations listed below, it is strongly recommended that you get advice from a lawyer before you decide to handle your divorce on your own. These situations can involve complex issues, and having a lawyer is the best way to protect your rights.

- You have been injured by your spouse and have a claim against him or her for money damages. This is known as a *Tevis claim*.
- There is a history of domestic violence against you or another family member. If you are a victim of domestic violence, you should be especially cautious once you file for divorce because that is a time when violence is likely to escalate or start again.
- You and your spouse disagree about who should have custody of the children.
- You and your spouse own real estate together.
- You and your spouse have real or personal property of significant value.
- You are receiving public benefits such as Temporary Assistance for Needy Families (TANF), General Assistance (GA), Emergency Assistance (EA), food stamps (FS), Medicaid, or Supplemental Security Income (SSI) and are concerned about how receiving alimony, property, or support from a divorce may affect your eligibility for those public benefits.
- You will be seeking alimony, also called spousal support.
- You or your spouse have a substantial pension.
- You or your spouse are involved in a personal injury lawsuit.
- You know the defendant is likely to hire or has hired a lawyer to contest the divorce or any agreements you have made.
- The defendant lives in a foreign country.
- The defendant is in the military.

Please note that it might be difficult to handle your own divorce if:
- You don't know where your spouse lives and you don't know anyone else who knows. (See the discussion on page 49 for serving your divorce complaint on a defendant whose whereabouts are unknown.)
- Your spouse is in the military or lives in a foreign country. A defendant who is in the military must have a lawyer representing him or her in a divorce. This manual does not provide instructions for handling a divorce when the defendant is in the military, and you should seek legal help if your spouse is in the military. Some information is provided on how to serve a defendant in a foreign country; however, you may want to seek legal help if the defendant does not live in the United States.

Dispute Resolution Alternatives

Dispute resolution alternatives are ways of settling lawsuits other than by trials or hearings. The primary forms of dispute resolution are mediation and arbitration. Parties in a divorce may also rely on other skilled financial professionals (such as accountants) or mental health professionals (such as psychologists) to resolve specific issues related to a divorce.

You may read more about dispute resolution alternatives by reviewing **Form 2A** on page 145 of this manual. You *must* get information about the alternate ways of settling lawsuits *before* you file your complaint or answer and counterclaim for divorce. The court now requires you to sign and file with your complaint or answer and counterclaim for divorce a special certification (sworn statement) claiming that you have received this information. (See *Certification of Notification of Complementary Dispute Resolution* (**Form 2B**) on page 147 of this manual.)

If there has been no domestic violence and you are comfortable meeting with your spouse and a third party to try to reach an agreement about property, support, custody, or parenting time (also called visitation) issues before you file your papers in court, you might consider seeking help from a mediator, arbitrator, or other skilled professional. Using the services of this independent third party to reach an agreement can save you money and time. Some mediators or arbitrators are also attorneys. However, an attorney who is acting as a mediator or arbitrator should never represent either of you in a divorce action and should not help you file for divorce. Even if you decide not to get a lawyer to represent you in your divorce, you and your spouse should each have your own lawyer review any settlement agreement that you reach through mediation or arbitration. Even if you resolve your differences through a dispute resolution alternative, you must still file papers with the court in order to get a divorce.

How Can I Get a Lawyer or Mediator to Help Me?

If you are a *low-income* New Jersey resident, you *may* be eligible for legal help from a Legal Services office in your area. See Appendix D on page 117 for a list of Legal Services programs in New Jersey. You may also be eligible for free legal advice from LSNJ-LAW™, Legal Services of New Jersey's statewide, toll-free legal hotline. The hotline telephone number is 1-888-LSNJ-LAW (1-888-576-5529). Hotline hours are Monday through Friday, 8 a.m. to 5:30 p.m. If you are not eligible for assistance from Legal Services, the hotline will refer you to other possible resources. To obtain a private lawyer, call the lawyer referral service of your county bar association. (See Appendix C on page 115 for the phone number of your county bar association's lawyer referral service.)

For more information about private mediators in New Jersey, call the New Jersey Association of Professional Mediators at 1-800-981-4800, or go to their Web site at *www.njapm.org/pg/home*. To learn more about court mediators, call (609) 984-4228 or go to *www.judiciary.state.nj.us/family/rosters/index.htm*.

Acknowledgments

For the first edition of this manual, Deborah Fennelly, senior attorney at LSNJ, did the research and initial writing, created all of the forms, and helped see the work through to conclusion. She made revisions and updates to this edition. Susan Perger, director of technology and publications, was responsible for editing, design, layout, and production. Special thanks to Maribel Whitfield, administrative assistant, for her help with the forms and to Tom Makin, LSNJ director of development and communications, and Tricia Simpson-Curtin for their help with editing and proofreading.

Comments or Suggestions

We hope that this manual will be helpful to you. Please let us know if you have comments or suggestions that we might use in future editions. You can write to us or e-mail us at:

Legal Services of New Jersey
P.O. Box 1357
Edison, NJ 08818-1357
publications@LSNJ.org

Melville D. Miller, Jr., President
Legal Services of New Jersey
Edison, New Jersey
June 2007

Introduction

How to Use This Manual

The suggestions below for using this manual will help you to decide whether you can handle the divorce on your own. If you decide to hire a lawyer, you will be clearer about what you want and more organized, which will save you and your lawyer time. See *Getting Legal Advice* on page 2 for a review of when you should seek legal assistance.

Read the Manual Carefully

Read the manual and examine the forms. Take notes while you are reading and write down any questions that come to mind. Some of your questions may be answered in this manual. You may want to ask a lawyer other questions. Make sure that you understand the information and the instructions for using the forms. You will find a glossary of legal terms mentioned in this manual on page 105.

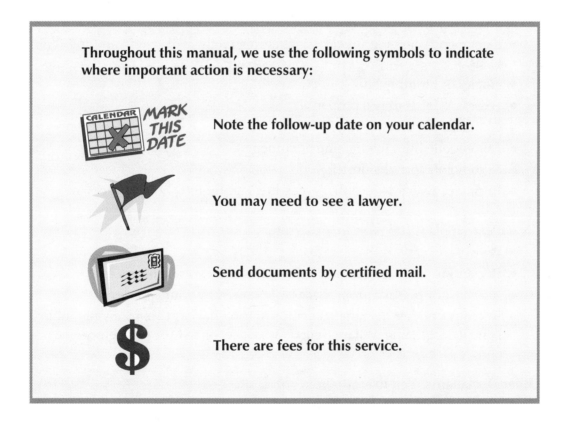

Throughout this manual, we use the following symbols to indicate where important action is necessary:

Note the follow-up date on your calendar.

You may need to see a lawyer.

Send documents by certified mail.

There are fees for this service.

Step 1: Gather Information and Records

After you have read the manual, you should gather together all of the documents that you will need to prepare your divorce papers. Then review the blank forms at the back of the manual and cut or tear out the ones that pertain to your situation. Before you begin to fill out the forms, we recommend that you make at least three copies of the blank forms so that you always have a clean copy to begin again if you make a mistake. Your finished forms must be 8 ½ x 11 inches and have straight edges. You will need all or most of the following documents and information for your divorce:

Any Court Orders Between You and Your Spouse Related to the Marriage. For example:
- Child support orders.
- Custody and parenting time/visitation orders.
- Name change orders.
- Domestic violence restraining orders and papers related to the domestic violence order, such as police or hospital reports.

Financial Information. This includes:
- Tax returns.
- Pay stubs and other proof of income (SSI, SSD, child support).
- List of bank accounts and copies of recent bank statements.
- Stocks, bonds, IRAs, and other financial assets.
- List of monthly expenses.
- Documents showing any debts, including credit card statements and loans.
- Copies of monthly bills.
- Leases or deeds to real property.
- Mortgage documents.
- Automobile titles (ownership documents).
- Automobile loan documents.
- Insurance policies—health, dental, life, automobile, homeowners, or rental.
- Pension plans and retirement accounts.
- Wills.
- Receipts for bills for personal injury caused by your spouse.
- Receipts for bills for property damage caused by your spouse.
- Receipts or other documents demonstrating that you are receiving public benefits, including welfare, rental assistance, or SSI for yourself or your children.

Other Documents. You may also need copies of:
- Your marriage certificate.
- Children's birth certificates.
- Children's Social Security numbers.

Make copies of these documents, and keep the original documents in a safe place. When you go to court for your divorce hearing, you may need to show the court some of these documents.

You will also need to have the following items as you move along in the divorce process:

- **A calendar for record keeping.** This is very important because there will be dates and deadlines that you will have to track.
- **Certified mail forms with return receipt cards.** Court rules require that some documents be sent by certified mail with a return receipt. *Certified mail* is a special mail service that provides proof of mailing at the time of mailing and date of delivery. The return receipt, which is signed by the recipient of the mail and sent back to you, provides information about the actual delivery of the mail. This return receipt will be part of your records and may have to be attached to certain documents. We recommend that, as part of your planning, you go to the post office and pick up several certified mail forms and return receipt cards. You should also get information about the cost of sending certified mail with a request for a return receipt so that you can plan for the mailing costs, which may be more than $3 each.

Step 2: Decide What You Want From the Divorce

This is an important step. Think very carefully about what you want to ask for in your divorce. **Remember:** The law requires that you raise all legal issues that you have against your spouse in your divorce complaint. Before you fill out the complaint forms, you need to decide what other relief you want in addition to having the court end your marriage. Looking at the information about your and your spouse's finances and property will help you decide what to ask for in your divorce. Below are things that you might ask for in your divorce complaint. They are explained in more detail in *Chapter 1: Preparing and Filing the Divorce Complaint* on page 19.

Alimony/Spousal Support. *Alimony*, also called *spousal support*, is money paid by one spouse to support the other spouse once the marriage has ended. Do you want to ask for alimony? If you are receiving public benefits and then begin to receive alimony, how will this affect your eligibility for those public benefits?

Division of Real Property. *Real property* refers to a house, a building, or a parcel of land. If you own your home, how do you want to divide it? Do you want your home sold immediately? Do you want to continue living in the home and, if so, for how long? If you are receiving public benefits, will this affect your eligibility for those public benefits?

Division of Personal Property. What will you do with *personal property*—cars, appliances, TV sets, sound equipment, jewelry, expensive tools, furniture, etc.?

Division of Debts. Who will be responsible for outstanding debts? This includes credit cards, loans, mortgages, car payments, outstanding rent and utility bills, etc.

Taking Back Your Former Name or Changing Your Name. Would you like to use another name? You may request this relief in your divorce complaint.

Insurance Policies and Premiums. Who will pay health, homeowners, or life insurance premiums? It is most likely that you will not be eligible for coverage on your spouse's health insurance policy once you are divorced.

Money Damages for Personal Injury. Have you been injured by your spouse? Has he or she damaged any property? If you are receiving public benefits (TANF, GA, EA, food stamps, Medicaid, SSI, etc.) and you receive money damages in the form of a personal injury award, how will this affect your eligibility for those public benefits?

Child Custody. With whom will the children live?

Parenting Time/Visitation. How often will visits take place? Where? What about holidays and vacations? Is supervised visitation necessary?

Child Support. If the children are remaining in your custody, how much child support should your spouse pay you? Will you need help with medical or dental expenses for your children? Who will provide health and dental insurance for the children? If you are receiving public benefits and you begin to receive child support, will this affect your eligibility for those public benefits or the amount of benefits that you receive?

Step 3: Prepare and Review Your Forms

There are different types of divorce claims. You may claim a specific reason or cause for your divorce. Or you may file a no-fault divorce and simply claim that the reason you want a divorce is that you and your spouse have experienced irreconcilable differences for six months or more or have been living separately for at least 18 months and there is no possibility of getting back together.

Once you know what kind of divorce you want and what kind of relief you want, you are ready to begin filling out the forms in this manual. We suggest that you make at least three copies of the blank forms so that you always have a clean copy to begin again if you make a mistake. The forms also can be completed on a typewriter. If necessary, you may fill them in by hand, but you must print clearly.

Proofread all of your forms carefully for accuracy. When you file papers with the court, you are giving your word that your statements are true and accurate. It is against the law to lie to the court. Remember that the law requires you to raise all legal issues that you have against your spouse and to ask for everything you want from your spouse in your divorce complaint. You will not be able to ask the judge at your divorce hearing for anything that you do not ask for in your divorce complaint, and you will not be able to bring a future lawsuit for things you do not put in your complaint. So check your complaint carefully before you file it with the court, to make sure that everything you want is contained in the complaint.

Time Requirements and Deadlines. You will need a calendar to keep track of many time requirements and deadlines. Pay attention to the deadlines, and always keep your case moving forward. Missing deadlines can have serious consequences. For example, the court can dismiss your case if you do not serve the defendant (give him or her a copy of your divorce complaint) within a certain time frame or if your reasons for not serving the defendant are not convincing. It is important to document all of your efforts to serve the defendant.

Other Suggestions

Before you file your papers with the court, you may want to see a lawyer for legal advice. (See *A Word of Caution about Using this Manual* on page 1, and *Getting Legal Advice* on page 2, where we strongly recommend that you talk to a lawyer in some specific circumstances. Please refer back to those pages now.)

Once you are satisfied that you understand what you may be entitled to in your divorce and how a divorce may affect any public benefits that you are receiving, you are ready to prepare and file your papers.

Appendix A on page 112 contains the addresses and telephone numbers of each county courthouse where you are required to file your divorce complaint. Addresses for county courthouses in New Jersey are also available on the Internet at *www.judiciary.state.nj.us/trial.htm*.

Flow Chart 1:
Overview of the Divorce Process

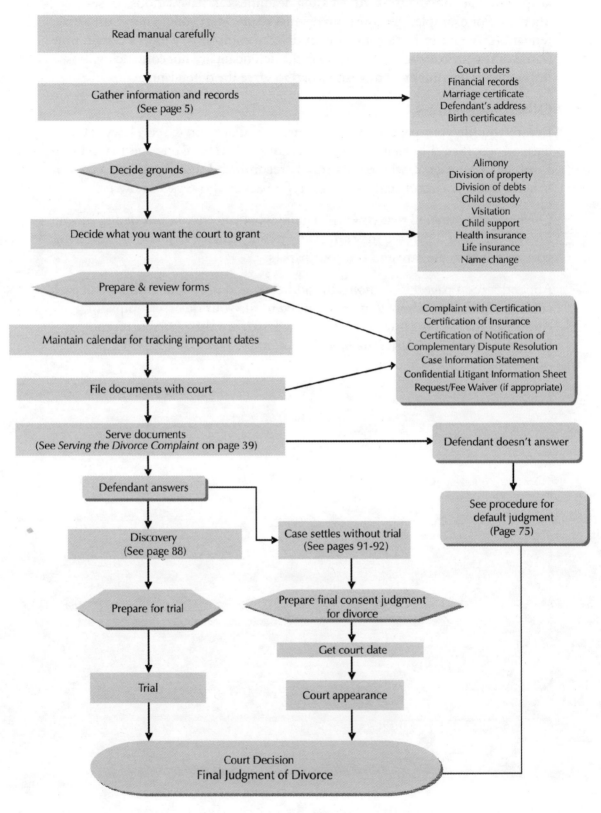

Read manual carefully

Gather information and records
(See page 5)

Court orders
Financial records
Marriage certificate
Defendant's address
Birth certificates

Decide grounds

Decide what you want the court to grant

Alimony
Division of property
Division of debts
Child custody
Visitation
Child support
Health insurance
Life insurance
Name change

Prepare & review forms

Maintain calendar for tracking important dates

Complaint with Certification
Certification of Insurance
Certification of Notification of
Complementary Dispute Resolution
Case Information Statement
Confidential Litigant Information Sheet
Request/Fee Waiver (if appropriate)

File documents with court

Serve documents
(See *Serving the Divorce Complaint* on page 39)

Defendant doesn't answer

Defendant answers

See procedure for
default judgment
(Page 75)

Discovery
(See page 88)

Case settles without trial
(See pages 91-92)

Prepare for trial

Prepare final consent judgment
for divorce

Get court date

Trial

Court appearance

Court Decision
Final Judgment of Divorce

Quick Reference to Forms in This Manual

On the following pages, we include a chapter-by-chapter listing of all of the forms in this manual. You will also find a table of forms at the end of each chapter.

colspan table		

Forms for Chapter 1: Preparing and Filing the Divorce Complaint
Forms 1 through 6

Form #	Title of Form	Instructions
1A, IB, 1C, or 1D	Complaint for Divorce and Attached Certification	Send original and two copies to court clerk for filing.
2	Certification of Insurance	Attach to complaint or answer and counterclaim. Send original and two copies to court clerk for filing.
2A	Explanation of Dispute Resolution Alternatives	Read this explanation before filling out and signing Form 2B. This form *should not* be filed with the court.
2B	Certification of Notification of Complementary Dispute Resolution	Read Form 2A before filling out this certification. Attach to complaint or answer and counterclaim. Send original and two copies to clerk for filing.
3A	Family Part Case Information Statement (CIS)	File with complaint in cases where there is any issue about custody, support, alimony, or equitable distribution. Make sure copies of pay stubs, tax returns, and other required documents are attached.
3B	Confidential Litigant Information Sheet (CLIS)	DO NOT attach to the complaint or any other document that you file with the court. This is a confidential document for use by court personnel only.
4 and 5, if applicable	Request for Waiver of Fees and Supporting Certification and Order Waiving Fees	Send original and two copies to court clerk for filing.
6	Filing Letter to Court	Submit to court with Forms 1-5 for filing. Keep a copy for your records.

Forms for Chapter 2: Serving the Divorce Complaint
Forms 7 through 12B

Form #	Title of Form	Instructions
Forms 7, 7A, and 7B—Personal Service on Defendant by Sheriff		
7 7A	Summons and Attached Proof of Service Cover Letter	Send original and two copies to sheriff's office with your complaint and all attached certifications. Keep a copy for your records. Sheriff will return proof of service when service is completed.
7B	Filing Letter to Court—Sheriff's Proof of Service	Submit to court clerk with original and two copies of completed Proof of Service (Form 7).
Forms 8, 8A, and 8B—Service by Mail on Cooperative Defendant		
8 8A	Acknowledgment of Service Cover Letter to Defendant or Defendant's Attorney	Send to defendant or defendant's attorney with Summons (Form 7) and copy of your complaint via regular *and* certified mail, return receipt requested. Keep a copy for your records.
8B	Filing Letter to Court—Acknowledgment of Service	Send original and two copies of signed and notarized Form 8 to court clerk for filing.
Forms 9 through 9H—Letters of Diligent Inquiry		
9	Letter of Inquiry to Defendant's Friends, Family, or Employers	Send original via regular *and* certified mail, return receipt requested. Keep a copy of each for your records.
9A	Letter of Inquiry to MVC	Same as for Form 9.
9B	Letter of Inquiry to Postmaster	Same as for Form 9.
9C	Letter of Inquiry to Military	Same as for Form 9.
9D	Letter of Inquiry to Military (Army)	Same as for Form 9.
9E	Letter of Inquiry to Military (Air Force)	Same as for Form 9.
9F	Letter of Inquiry to Military (Navy)	Same as for Form 9.
9G	Letter of Inquiry to Military (Marine Corps)	Same as for Form 9.
9H	Letter of Inquiry to Military (Coast Guard)	Same as for Form 9.

Forms 10A, 10B, and 10C—Substituted Service on Special Agent		
10A	Request for Order Permitting Substituted Service on a Special Agent and Supporting Certification	Send original and two copies to the court clerk for filing along with Form 10B. Attach copies of letters of inquiry (Forms 9-9H) and replies, if any, to supporting certification.
10B	Order Permitting Substituted Service on a Special Agent	Send original and two copies to the court clerk for filing along with Form 10A.
10C	Filing Letter to Court—Request for Substituted Service	Send to the court with Forms 10A and 10B. Keep a copy for your records.
Forms 11A through 12B—Service by Publication		
11A	Request for Order Permitting Service by Publication and Supporting Certification	Send original and two copies to the court for filing along with Form 11B. Attach copies of letters of inquiry (Forms 9-9H) and replies, if any, to supporting certification.
11B	Order Permitting Service by Publication	Send original and two copies to the court for filing along with Form 11A.
11C	Filing Letter to Court—Request for Service by Publication	Send to the court with Forms 11A and 11B. Keep a copy for your records.
12	Notice of Order of Publication	Send to newspaper after you receive signed order (Form 11B). Keep a copy for your records.
12A	Cover Letter to Newspaper Requesting Publication	Send to newspaper with Form 12. Keep a copy for your records.
12B	Filing Letter to Court Re: Certification of Publication	Send with an original and two copies of certification of publication from newspaper to the court for filing. Keep a copy for your records.

Forms for Chapter 3: After Serving the Divorce Complaint
Forms 13 through 16

Form #	Title of Form	Instructions
Documents to Be Filed by a Defendant—Forms 4 & 5 and Forms 13 through 14E		
4 and 5, if applicable	Request for Waiver of Fees and Supporting Certification, and Order Waiving Fees	Send original and two copies to court clerk for filing.
13	Consent Order Extending Time to Answer	Send original and two copies to court clerk for filing.
13A	Filing Letter to Court—Consent Order Extending Time to Answer	Send to court clerk with Form 13.
14A, 14B, 14C, or 14D	Answer and Counterclaim for Divorce and Attached Certification	Send original and two copies to court clerk for filing, along with Forms 2 and 2B. **In cases where there is any issue as to custody, support, alimony, or equitable distribution,** send Forms 3A and 3B to court clerk for filing within 20 days after filing answer.
14E	Filing Letter to Court—Answer and Counterclaim for Divorce	Send to court clerk with Form 14A, 14B, 14C, or 14D, and Forms 2, 2B, and 16.
Documents Plaintiff Files if Defendant Submits an Answer and Counterclaim to Divorce—Forms 15A through 16		
15A	Answer to Counterclaim for Divorce	Send original and two copies to court clerk for filing along with Form 16.
15B	Filing Letter to Court—Answer to Counterclaim for Divorce	Send with Forms 15A and 16.
16	Certification of Service	Send with specific designated forms (see above and below).

Forms for Chapter 4: Getting a Default Judgment
Forms 17 through 21A

Form #	Title of Form	Instructions
Documents to Be Filed When Defendant Is in Default		
17	Request to Enter Default Judgment and Supporting Certification and Certification of Service (Form 16)	Send original and two copies to court for filing. At the same time, send one copy of each form to defendant via regular *and* certified mail, return receipt requested.
17A	Filing Letter to Court—Request to Enter Default Judgment	Send to court with Forms 16, 17, and 18. Keep a copy for your records.
18	Certification of Non-Military Service (attach certificates from each branch of the military)	Send to court with Forms 16, 17, and 17A for filing. At the same time, send one copy to defendant via regular *and* certified mail, return receipt requested.
19	Notice of Default Divorce Hearing and Certification of Service (Form 16)	Send to defendant via regular *and* certified mail, return receipt requested. Keep a copy for your records.
19A	Cover Letter to Defendant—Notice of Default Divorce Hearing	Send to defendant via regular *and* certified mail, return receipt requested, with Form 20. Keep a copy for your records.
20	Notice of Application for Equitable Distribution and Certification of Service (Form 16)	**20 days or more before the date of your divorce hearing**, submit an original and one copy to the court for filing, along with Form 16. **Send to defendant via regular *and* certified mail, return receipt requested, in time to ensure that defendant receives the document 20 days or more prior to the hearing.**
20A	Filing Letter to Court—Notice of Application for Equitable Distribution	Send to defendant with Forms 20 and 16. Keep a copy for your records.
21	Final Default Judgment of Divorce	Bring to court on day of default hearing. Judge will probably sign and file it **in court on that day**. Send filed copy to defendant with Form 16 within seven days of the date it is signed by the judge. File form 16 with the court. Keep a copy for your records.
21A	Cover Letter to Defendant—Final Default Judgment of Divorce	Send to defendant with Form 21. Keep a copy for your records.

Forms for Chapter 5: Going to Court When Defendant Is Not in Default
Forms 22 through 26A

Form #	Title of Form	Instructions
22	Custody and Parenting Time/Visitation Plan	**75 days or less after the answer or (if there is one) answer to counter-claim is filed,** submit original and one copy to court for filing. Send a copy to the other parent via regular *and* certified mail, return receipt requested, with Form 16.
22A	Filing Letter to Court—Custody and Parenting Time/Visitation Plan	Send to court with Form 22. Send a copy to other parent with copy of Form 22.
23	Subpoena Duces Tecum ad Testificandum	Send a copy to witness via regular *and* certified mail, return receipt requested, with fee (see page 94). Keep a copy for your records.
23A	Cover Letter to Witness—Subpoena Duces Tecum ad Testificandum	Send to witness via regular *and* certified mail, return receipt requested, with Form 23.
24	Consent Order—Final Judgment of Divorce	Send filed copy to ex-spouse via certified or regular mail along with Form 16 within seven days of the date that it is signed by the judge. Keep a copy for your records.
25	Final Judgment of Divorce	Send filed copy to ex-spouse via certified or regular mail, along with Form 16, within seven days of the date that it is signed by the judge. Keep a copy for your records.
26	Cover Letter to Judge—Five-Day Rule	If court instructs one party to prepare another order, send to the court as soon as possible after hearing and send copy to spouse.
26A	Cover Letter—Final Judgment of Divorce	Send to court with Form 26. Send copy to spouse. Instructs spouse that he or she has five days within which to give the court notice of his or her objections to the form of the order. If there are no objections, the court will sign and file. After signed and sent to preparing party, preparing party should send a copy to ex-spouse within seven days of date order was signed.

Chapter 1:
Preparing and Filing the Divorce Complaint

This chapter will show you how to:

- Prepare the divorce complaint and additional documents.
- File your divorce complaint and other documents with the court.
- Pay filing fees and other costs.
- Keep track of time limits and deadlines.

This chapter will cover Forms 1 through 6.

Chapter 1:
Preparing and Filing the Divorce Complaint

Types of Divorce

New Jersey has both a *no-fault divorce* and a *fault-based divorce*. You will find forms for four kinds of divorce in this manual: forms for a no-fault divorce, based on 18-month separation (**Form 1A**) and based on irreconcilable differences (**Form 1D**), and forms for two fault-based divorces, based on desertion (**Form 1B**) and based on extreme cruelty (**Form 1C**).

This chapter will explain how to prepare and file your divorce complaint (**Form 1A, 1B, 1C, or 1D**) and file it with the court. We suggest that, as you read this chapter, you look at the complaint form (**Form 1A, 1B, 1C, or 1D**) that you will be using for your divorce. Also look at **Forms 2** through **6**, which you also must complete and send to the court with your complaint.

No-Fault Divorce

No-fault divorce means that the court will end the marriage based on separation (the fact that you and your spouse have been living in different places for 18 consecutive months or more), or based on irreconcilable differences (the fact that you and your spouse have experienced irreconcilable differences for a period of six months or more). The advantage of getting a no-fault divorce is that the law does not require proof that either spouse was responsible for causing the marriage to end. See ***Complaint for Divorce Based on Separation and Attached Certification*** (**Form 1A**) and ***Complaint for Divorce Based on Irreconcilable Differences and Attached Certification*** (**Form 1D**).

To file a no-fault divorce complaint in New Jersey based on separation, the following requirements must be met:
- You or your spouse must have lived in New Jersey for 12 consecutive months preceding the filing of the divorce complaint.
- You and your spouse must have lived apart—that means in separate residences—for at least 18 consecutive months before beginning the divorce action.
- There is no reasonable prospect of reconciliation.

To file a no-fault divorce complaint based on irreconcilable differences in New Jersey, the following requirements must be met:
- You or your spouse must have lived in New Jersey for 12 consecutive months preceding the filing of the divorce complaint.
- You and your spouse must have experienced irreconcilable differences for a period of six months.

- The irreconcilable differences make it appear that the marriage should be dissolved.
- There is no reasonable prospect of reconciliation.

Fault-Based Divorce

The other type of divorce action is a divorce based on a specific reason (ground or fault). This manual will explain how to do fault-based divorces based on desertion and extreme cruelty. Desertion and extreme cruelty are among the most common grounds for a fault-based divorce.

Desertion. Desertion occurs when one spouse leaves the other spouse for 12 months or more against the wishes of the other spouse. A party must wait until he or she has been deserted for at least 12 months before he or she can file a complaint for divorce based on desertion. See *Complaint for Divorce Based on Desertion and Attached Certification* **(Form 1B)**. To file a divorce complaint based on desertion, the following basic requirements must be met:

- You or your spouse must have lived in New Jersey for the 12 consecutive months preceding the filing of the divorce complaint.
- Your spouse must have deserted you for 12 months or more against your will.

Extreme Cruelty. Extreme cruelty includes acts of cruelty that range from unpleasantness and emotional abuse to those involving severe physical violence. See *Complaint for Divorce Based on Extreme Cruelty and Attached Certification* **(Form 1C)**. To file a divorce based on extreme cruelty, the following basic requirements must be met:

- You or your spouse must have lived in New Jersey for the 12 consecutive months preceding the filing of the divorce complaint.
- The most recent acts of cruelty you claim in the complaint must have happened at least three months before you file the complaint for divorce. For example, if you file your divorce complaint on June 1, 2007, the last act of extreme cruelty that you should put in your complaint is an event that occurred on or before February 28, 2007. This is true even if the cruelty is still going on when you file the complaint. Include all acts of abuse that occurred from the day you were married until the date that is three months before the date you sign your divorce complaint. If the abuse is ongoing, you will simply leave out the specific acts that happened in the last three months before you file.

Other Fault-Based Grounds. Other fault-based grounds include adultery, deviant sexual conduct, habitual drunkenness or voluntary addiction to any narcotic drugs, institutionalization for mental illness, and incarceration. This manual does not provide information for divorces based on those grounds.

Preparing Your Divorce Complaint

The complaint is the document that begins your case and presents your situation to the court. The complaint also contains what you are asking the court to order. This is called *legal relief*.

Information Required by the Court

The following is a short list of the information that should appear in your complaint.

- The names and addresses of you and your spouse. (See paragraphs 1 and 6 on the complaint.)

  Note to victims of domestic violence: If you are hiding from your spouse because you are afraid, you do not have to write your street address and phone number in the body of the complaint. (See paragraphs 1, 5, and 6 on **Forms 1A** and **1B;** paragraphs 1, 6, and 7 on **Form 1C**; and paragraphs 1, 9, and 10 on **Form 1D**.) If you are afraid to disclose your address, you will need to provide a post office box number or an alternative address where you can receive mail. You should consider obtaining this alternative address through the New Jersey Address Confidentiality Program (ACP), which is a program designed to help victims of domestic violence who have relocated for their safety. The program limits the abuser's access to information that would reveal the victim's new location and allows the victim to receive first-class mail by way of the New Jersey Department of Community Affairs. For further information about the ACP or to register for the program, call 1-877-218-9133 or visit this Web site: ***www.njcbw.org/legaladdress.htm***. You may also register as a participant in the program by contacting your county domestic violence program. For the address or phone number of your county domestic violence program, call the New Jersey Coalition for Battered Women at 1-609-584-8107 or visit the Coalition Web site: ***www.njcbw.org*** or ***www.nj.gov/dca/dow/countyresources.shtml***. Your alternative address goes on the top of the complaint so that the court can contact you. Depending upon the particular facts of your case, the court rules will require you to file your complaint in a county where you or your spouse now lives. (See page 31 for details about how to determine where to properly file your complaint.) If the rules require you to file your complaint in the county where you now live and you don't feel safe even having your spouse know which county you live in, you should apply for an alternative address through the Address Confidentiality Program described above.

- The date of your marriage. (See paragraph 2.)
- The reason you are seeking or grounds on which you are basing a divorce. If you are seeking a no-fault divorce, you must state the date you and your spouse began to live separately, and where you lived when you separated. If you are seeking a fault divorce based on extreme cruelty, you must describe the acts of cruelty on which you are basing your com-

plaint. List the dates of all acts of abuse that occurred from the day you were married until the date that is three months before you sign and date your divorce complaint. (See paragraph 3.)

- Confirmation that you have met the one-year residency requirement. (See paragraph 4 on **Forms 1A** and **1B**, paragraph 5 on **Form 1C**, and paragraph 8 on **Form 1D**.)

- Where you lived when you had been separated from the defendant for 18 months (see paragraph 5 on **Form 1A**), or when the defendant had deserted you for 12 months (see paragraph 5 on **Form 1B**), or when the defendant committed acts of cruelty against you (see paragraph 6 on **Form 1C**), or when you and the defendant had experienced irreconcilable differences for a period of six months (see paragraph 9 on **Form 1D**).

- The names and ages of any children. (See paragraph 7 on **Forms 1A** and **1B**, paragraph 8 on **Form 1C**, and paragraph 11 on **Form 1D**.)

- A list of any prior court actions between you and your spouse in New Jersey or in any other state where you lived—this could include court orders for adoption of children, child support, custody, visitation, or domestic violence restraining orders. Make sure to include the docket numbers of those court actions. (See paragraph 8 on **Forms 1A** and **1B**, paragraph 9 on **Form IC**, and paragraph 12 on **Form 1D**.)

- The relief you seek besides the divorce, such as custody, parenting time, alimony/spousal support, child support, or permission to use another name. (See the "WHEREFORE" clause of the complaint—**Forms 1A, 1B, 1C,** and **1D**.) *Remember:* This is an important part of your complaint. If there is anything that you want the court to order as a part of your divorce, you must make a general request for it in this section of your complaint. For example, if you are seeking spousal support or child support, you do not need to specify a dollar amount, but you do need to let the court know that you are requesting support. You and your spouse will agree to the specific amount in a settlement agreement or the judge will make a decision later.

At the end of the complaint (**Forms 1A, 1B, 1C,** and **1D**) is an additional statement, called a *Certification of Verification and Non-Collusion*, which you must sign. It states that you are making your complaint in good faith, that all the claims are true, that there are no other pending actions involving your marriage, and that no other people need to be included in this case.

Now is a good time to review all of the documents you gathered together relating to your marriage to help you decide what legal relief you will be asking for in your complaint.

Types of Relief

You must decide what you want and ask for those things in your divorce complaint. For example, you can ask the court to:

- Grant *alimony* (also called *spousal support*). When you complete your complaint, you only need to make a general request for alimony/spousal support. You do not need to specify a dollar amount at this time.
- Divide property (also called *equitable distribution*):
  - Divide *personal property* (such as furniture or cars);
  - Divide *real property* (such as a house or land); and
  - Divide debts.

  You do not need to specify the details concerning division of property in your complaint.
- Allow you to change your name.
- Order that one or both parties have custody of the minor children.
- Order that one or both parties have parenting time/visitation with the children. Once again, this is a general request. You do not need to specify the details concerning custody or parenting time/visitation.
- Order child support. You do not need to specify a dollar amount in the complaint, but you do need to make a general request.

Alimony/Spousal Support

Alimony refers to support paid by one spouse to the other to help the other spouse continue to live the way he or she lived while married. Alimony may be awarded to either party in a divorce action. The rules of alimony apply to both parties regardless of gender. Keep in mind that receiving alimony may affect your eligibility for public benefits. Please see *Important Information About Doing Your Own Divorce* on page 1.

There are several different types of alimony.

- **Permanent alimony.** Generally, permanent alimony is awarded only if the parties have been married for a very substantial time period, or if you are financially dependent or permanently unable to work because of disability or lack of skills or work experience. You may get alimony for the rest of your life or until you remarry. Either party may apply to the court after the divorce to adjust the amount of alimony when there has been a change in the parties' circumstances.
- **Limited duration alimony.** You may get temporary alimony until the occurrence of a particular event, such as when you get a job. In determining how long to grant alimony, the court must consider how long it will take you to improve your earning capacity so that alimony is no longer needed. The court can change the award based on changed circumstances or if the expected event does not occur. The court can change the amount of the award but will rarely change the length of time for alimony to be paid.

- **Rehabilitative alimony.** You will probably get temporary rehabilitative alimony if you are likely to be able to support yourself after more education or training. You must show the specific steps for rehabilitation and the amount of time they are expected to take. This type of alimony can also be changed based upon changed circumstances.
- **Reimbursement alimony.** You can get this type of alimony if you supported your spouse through school or training and expected to benefit from your spouse's increased income after finishing school.

In deciding whether or not to award alimony, the court should consider a number of factors. These include:

- The parties' actual needs and ability to pay.
- The length of the marriage.
- The age and physical and emotional health of both parties.
- The standard of living established during the marriage and the parties' abilities to maintain a reasonably comparable standard of living.
- The parties' earning capacities, educational levels, vocational skills, and employability.
- The length of time the party seeking alimony has been out of the job market.
- The parental responsibilities of the party seeking alimony.
- Each party's financial or non-financial contributions to the marriage.
- Any other income available to the parties.
- The equitable distribution of property and debts.
- The tax consequences of any alimony award.
- Any other factors the court finds relevant.

Equitable Distribution

Equitable distribution refers to how to divide property and debts that were incurred during the marriage between the parties under New Jersey divorce laws. Property and debts are not automatically divided 50/50, although they sometimes are. In dividing property, the judge will decide what is fair. If you have a substantial amount of property, you will probably want to consult with a lawyer about equitable distribution.

Normally, decisions about dividing property and debts cannot be changed after the judgment of divorce. In unusual cases, you may be able to get a change if you can show the court that there is a very good reason to change the decision.

Equitable Distribution of Marital Property. Equitable distribution applies only to what the court considers "marital property." Marital property is defined as property acquired by either party during the time between the date of their marriage and the filing of a divorce complaint, with some exceptions. Generally, gifts received by one spouse from a third party and property a relative leaves to one spouse in a will are not considered marital property, as long as they are kept independent from the other spouse (not put into a joint bank account or deed in the name of the other spouse). However, a gift from one spouse to another is considered to be marital property subject to equitable distribution.

Warning: If you and your spouse have property, you may want to consult a lawyer. Also keep in mind that, if you receive property or money from your divorce, this may affect your eligibility for public benefits.

Marital property can include:
- Real property (a house or land).
- Personal property (furniture or cars).
- Severance pay, pensions (even though you may not receive the money until sometime in the future), and personal injury awards.

In deciding the issue of equitable distribution of marital property, the judge must do the following:
- Decide what property is marital property.
- Determine the value of each piece of property to be divided.
- Determine how the property will be divided between the parties.

Equitable Distribution of Marital Debt. Marital debt is defined as any debt brought about by either party between the date of their marriage and the filing of a divorce complaint. However, the court may not consider all debt acquired during that time to be marital debt. Debt that comes from purchasing items not related to the marriage, especially purchases made after a separation, may not be subject to equitable distribution. In that situation, the court will often decide that only the spouse who incurs that non-marital debt is responsible for it.

Warning: See a lawyer if you or your spouse has significant debt.

In deciding the issue of equitable distribution of marital debt, the judge must do the following:
- Decide what debt is marital debt.
- Decide how much debt each party will be responsible for.

Generally, if the parties incur debts during the marriage, they are both potentially responsible for it. However, it may be possible to prove that a debt belongs to only one party. The other party will have to show that the debt happened after the parties stopped living together, or that the debt is for items unrelated to the parties' relationship.

Warning: If you are separated, and your spouse is authorized to use your credit card, you will probably want to cancel that authorization even before your divorce is final.

In deciding how to divide property and debts, the court must look at a number of factors, including:
- The length of the marriage.
- The age and physical and emotional health of both parties.
- The income or property each party brought to the marriage.
- The parties' current economic circumstances.
- Any written agreement between the parties concerning property distribution.
- The custodial parent's need to own or use the parties' home and household items.
- Expected future medical or educational costs for a spouse or child.
- Any other factors the court finds relevant.

Special Considerations

Pensions and Retirement Accounts. If you or your spouse has a pension, you will probably want to consult a lawyer. To divide a pension, you will need to get a special evaluation. A pension expert must estimate the value of the pension at the time it will be paid and tell the court how to determine the amount of the pension that should go to the other spouse. The expert will prepare a Qualified Domestic Relations Order (QDRO), which will explain how to divide the pension. This order must be approved by the court. The portion of the pension that goes to the other spouse is usually based on the number of years the parties were married.

Health Insurance. If your spouse works for an employer with 20 or more employees and his or her employer provides him or her with group health benefits, you can request that your spouse continue to cover you under his or her insurance policy for a limited time after the divorce. The law that requires employers to offer this continuation or extension of health coverage in certain instances where coverage under that plan would normally end is known as *COBRA*, which stands for Consolidated Omnibus Reconciliation Act of 1986, the official title of that federal law. If your spouse's employer does not have health insurance, or is not covered by COBRA, you can request that the court order that he or she pay for the cost of insurance for you and your children.

Personal Injury Awards. If one party was injured during the marriage, the other party may be entitled to a portion of any personal injury award based on lost earnings. This may be true even if the award is not received until after the parties are divorced. This may be the type of situation where you will need the services of an attorney in order to actually receive what you are entitled to receive. (See *Getting Legal Advice* on page 2.) Keep in mind that receiving a personal injury award may affect your eligibility for public benefits.

Taking Back Your Former Name or Changing Your Name. When you get a divorce, the judge may allow either spouse to resume a former name or to take a new name. If this relief is granted, you are not required to begin using the new name. If you want to use the new name, you will need to show your final judgment to agencies such as the Motor Vehicle Commission, Social Security, and your bank.

Relief Available for People With Children

If you have children, you will probably need to ask for additional relief in your divorce complaint concerning custody of the children, parenting time/visitation, and child support.

Custody. If you and your spouse do not agree about child custody, the judge will have to decide this in the divorce case. The judge must decide what custody arrangement is in the child's best interests. If you have serious concerns about who will get custody, you should talk to a lawyer.

There are two aspects of custody: legal custody and physical custody. The parent with primary legal custody is responsible for making important decisions concerning the child, such as where the child should go to school and what kind of medical care the child should get. The parent with primary physical custody is the parent the child lives with most of the time. This parent is called the *custodial parent*, and the other parent is called the *non-custodial parent*. Parents can also share custody jointly.

- **Joint physical custody** (also called shared physical custody). The child lives with each parent for similar amounts of time during the year. In this situation, both parents have day-to-day responsibility for the child.
- **Primary physical custody.** The child lives most of the time with one parent. The other parent may visit the child.
- **Joint legal custody.** Both parents are involved in making important decisions concerning the child's education, medical care, and similar issues. Both have access to the child's school and medical records.
- **Primary legal custody.** Only one parent is responsible for making important decisions concerning the child.

Custody arrangements can vary greatly, depending upon the needs of the children and the relationship of the parents. The court does not have to give both parents physical and legal custody. Often the parties have joint legal custody, but one party has primary physical custody. In some very rare situations, one parent will get legal and physical custody. This parent is said to have *sole custody*. Sole custody is ordered only where one parent is missing, absent, or found to be legally "unfit."

Custody decisions are based on the child's best interests. The court will look at a number of factors, including:

- The parents' ability to agree, communicate, and cooperate.
- The child's relationship with the parents and siblings.

- Any history of domestic violence.
- The child's safety, needs, and preference.
- Each parent's ability to take care of the child.
- The child's education.
- The amount of time each parent has spent with the child.
- The parents' employment responsibilities.
- The ages and number of children.
- Any other factors the court finds relevant.

Decisions involving custody can be changed by the court if the parties' or children's circumstances change.

Other issues around custody include the following:

- **Parent education.** In every divorce action where custody, visitation, or support of a minor child or children is an issue, the court will order the parents to attend a Parents' Education Program to be offered twice a month through the court. There is a $25 fee to attend this program, and attendance is mandatory. The program is designed to assist and advise divorcing parents on issues concerning divorce, separation, and custody, to promote cooperation between them and assist them in resolving issues concerning their children that may arise during the divorce or separation process. The court may exempt a party from attending this program if a temporary or final restraining order, restraining either party from contact with the other, has been issued or for other good cause determined by the court.

- **Custody mediation.** When there is a dispute about custody or parenting time, the court will usually refer the parties to mediation to see if a court mediator can help resolve the issue. If a temporary or final domestic violence restraining order has been entered against you or your spouse, you cannot be required to participate in mediation. Likewise, if there are issues of child abuse or sexual abuse, the case will not be mediated. If circumstances require it, even after mediation has begun, the mediator or either party can petition the court for permission to remove the case from mediation by demonstrating good cause for removal. If an agreement is reached, it is memorialized in writing and a copy is given to each party. If an agreement is not reached, the case goes back to the court to be settled by way of a trial or hearing.

- **Court investigations.** The court can ask the probation division or other court staff to conduct an investigation of the parties and their homes and file a report with the court. This is sometimes referred to as a *best interests investigation*.

- **Parenting plans.** Unless you and your spouse agree about custody, you will both have to file a ***Custody and Parenting Time/Visitation Plan (Form 22)*** with the court within 75 days of the date the defendant answers the complaint. If the defendant files a counterclaim, you will need to file your plan within 75 days of filing your answer to the counter-claim. (See *Custody and Parenting Time/Visitation Plan* on page 90.)

Parenting Time/Visitation. The non-custodial parent will almost always have visits or parenting time with the child. Visits will only be restricted if the court believes that the non-custodial parent will harm the child. Decisions about visitation are based on what is best for the child. Visitation can be changed if the parties' or children's circumstances change.

Child Support. Both parents have a duty to financially support their children. Child support is financial support provided by the non-custodial parent to the custodial parent to help support the children. Child support decisions are based on New Jersey's Child Support Guidelines, which have detailed rules for deciding how much support a parent should pay. The amount of child support ordered will depend upon the parents' incomes, the number of children, and other factors. The child support award should include money to help pay for childcare expenses. In addition to child support, the court should make certain that the parties provide health insurance for the child. The guidelines are in the *New Jersey Court Rules*. The county law library in your county courthouse will most probably have a copy. Your local library may have a copy. If not, the librarian can help you find a copy. You can also read the guidelines on the New Jersey Judiciary Web site at ***www.judiciary.state.nj.us/csguide/index.htm***.

Keep in mind that receiving child support may affect your eligibility for public benefits. Please see *Important Information About Doing Your Own Divorce* on page 1.

Other Documents to Be Filed With the Complaint

The complaint must be filed with other documents. You should make five photocopies of every document you prepare. You will then send the original and two copies to the court and keep the extra two copies for your records and for later use. Once you send your papers to the court and you have received a docket number and a copy marked "filed," you will have to write the docket number on all of your photocopies. You should also make three copies of each filed document. You may need to use these copies later.

Always include a self-addressed, stamped envelope (an envelope that has both postage and your name and address) with any documents that you send to the court so that the court can send you back a copy marked filed. You should do this even if you hand-deliver your papers to the court. You may need to know the date on which the court received something, and the filed document will have the date, time, and location of the filing on it.

All of the documents that you have to file with the complaint are explained in detail below. Please look at the forms as you read the instructions.
- *Filing Letter to Court—Complaint* **(Form 6).** Your filing letter must let the court know what you are sending and request a filed copy of the complaint and the other documents that accompany it. The filing letter

must indicate whether you are paying the filing fee or seeking a fee waiver (which will only be given if you cannot afford the filing fee), as explained on page 33. Make sure to check off all appropriate statements.

- ***Certification of Verification and Non-Collusion*** (attached to complaint). This is a sworn statement that appears at the end of your complaint (**Form 1A, 1B, 1C,** or **1D**). It lets the court know that:

  o All of the claims and facts in the complaint are true.

  o There is no other divorce action, or any other legal matter involving you or your spouse, presently filed in any court or arbitration proceeding. If there is some other legal matter involving you and your spouse, you must let the court know what it is.

  o There are no other people who should be included in this divorce.

  You have a continuing obligation to update this information if it changes during the time that the divorce is pending in court. If the information is untrue or is not updated, the court may dismiss your complaint.

- ***Certification of Insurance*** (**Form 2**). This is a separate form that must be attached to your divorce complaint. It lists all known insurance coverage for you, your spouse, and your minor children. This includes life, health, automobile, and homeowners insurance. Any insurance coverage identified in the certification of insurance at the time the complaint is filed must be maintained until the court orders otherwise. If you do not file this document with your complaint, the clerk may refuse to file your complaint.

- ***Certification of Notification of Complementary Dispute Resolution*** (**Form 2B**). This is another separate form that must be attached to your divorce complaint. It states that you have been informed about dispute resolution alternatives that you may use to settle your case. Before you sign this document, you must read the information contained in ***Explanation of Dispute Resolution Alternatives*** (**Form 2A**) found on page 145 of this manual.

- ***Family Part Case Information Statement (CIS)*** (**Form 3A**). This must be filed with your divorce complaint if there is an issue of custody, support, alimony, or division of property and debt (*equitable distribution*). Even if you are not seeking these types of relief, the court may require you to complete a CIS. The CIS asks for detailed information about the financial circumstances, income, and assets of each party. The financial papers you gathered during your planning will help you give accurate information to the court about your financial circumstances. You will also have to photocopy and attach some financial documents to this form, such as tax returns and pay stubs. See the instructions on this form. It is important that this information be accurate and true.

  You are required to update your CIS when and if anything changes before the divorce is final. If the court finds that the information you provided in your CIS is untrue or has not been updated, the court could dismiss your complaint or prohibit you from introducing evidence of any assets that were not listed on your CIS.

If you and your husband or wife come to an agreement or settlement that includes an award of alimony, the court rules require both of you to preserve a copy of your respective Family CIS until alimony is terminated. (The final judgment of divorce will tell both of you when alimony is to end either by giving a specific time period for alimony, or by stating that alimony will end when a certain event happens, such as the remarriage of the former husband or wife.)

If you and your husband or wife come to an agreement or settlement that includes an award of alimony and you have not filed a Family CIS, the court rules require both of you to prepare at least Part D (monthly expenses) of the Family CIS, serve a copy on each other and, once again, preserve a copy of the completed Part D until alimony is terminated.

- **Confidential Litigant Information Sheet (CLIS)** **(Form 3B).** This is a form that the court requires you to fill out and file when you file your divorce complaint if you are requesting alimony or child support as relief in your complaint. The CLIS is to be filed separately and *is not* to be attached to the complaint or to any other document that is filed as a public record. The CLIS provides the court with relevant updated personal information for the court's use in establishing, modifying, or enforcing support orders. The personal information is to be used solely as a means to update the official state computer system and to provide the court with the ability to contact you if necessary. The information contained in the CLIS is to be used only by the *state* and *only* for the purpose of *contacting you about your child support or alimony case.* The CLIS is a confidential document. This means that it is not a public record and should not be shared with any member of the public.

    Note to victims of domestic violence: To ensure your safety, if you are hiding from your spouse, you should consider obtaining an alternative address through the New Jersey Address Confidentiality Program (see page 21).

- **Request for Waiver of Fees and Supporting Certification** **(Form 4)** and **Order Waiving Fees** **(Form 5).** If you cannot afford the filing fees, file **Forms 4** and **5** to get permission from the court to waive the fees. (This is explained under *Filing the Complaint with the Court* below.) You will not fill out **Forms 4** and **5** if you *can* afford the fees for filing (and for the Parents' Education Program if you and your spouse have children). You will simply pay the fees by check when you file your papers. You will have to call the court clerk to find out the amount of these fees.

- **A self-addressed, stamped envelope.** On the front of your package to the court, you should enclose an envelope containing postage and your name and address so the court can return a filed copy of the papers to you. It is very important that you have copies of your documents marked filed. You will need them for your records and for later use. The court will not send you copies of the filed documents unless you provide the self-addressed, stamped envelope.

Filing the Complaint With the Court

Where to File Your Complaint

Where you choose to file your divorce complaint is controlled by the *New Jersey Court Rules*. These rules require you to first determine when your *cause of action* (the grounds or reason) for your divorce arose. A cause of action is said to have "arisen" when the facts of your situation meet the requirements for that cause of action. For example, if you are filing a divorce complaint based on separation, your cause of action for separation is said to have arisen at the point when you and your spouse had lived separate and apart from each other for 18 months. If you are filing your divorce complaint based on desertion, your cause of action for desertion is said to have arisen at the point when your spouse had willingly deserted you for 12 months. If you are filing your divorce complaint based on extreme cruelty, your cause of action is said to have arisen three months after the date of the last act of cruelty that your spouse committed against you as described in your complaint. The rules then require you to determine, if possible, where you were living at the time that your cause of action for divorce arose. (See Appendix A on page 112 for county court addresses.)

- **If you were living in New Jersey at the time that your cause of action for divorce arose and you are now living in New Jersey.** You must file the complaint in the county where you lived at the time that your cause of action for divorce arose, even if you now live in a different New Jersey county. (For example, if you were living in Somerset County, New Jersey, at the time that your cause of action arose but you now live in Camden County, you must file your complaint in Somerset County.)

- **If you were living outside of New Jersey at the time that your cause of action for divorce arose but your spouse was living in New Jersey at that time.** You must file your divorce complaint in the New Jersey county where your spouse was living when the cause of action arose. (For example, if you lived in Connecticut at the time that your cause of action for divorce arose and your spouse was living in Somerset County in New Jersey at that time, you must file your complaint in Somerset County.)

- **If both you and your spouse were living outside of New Jersey at the time that your cause of action for divorce arose and you now live in New Jersey.** You must file your complaint in the New Jersey county in which you are now living. (For example, at the time that your cause of action for divorce arose, you and your spouse were living in Connecticut and you now live in Somerset County, New Jersey; regardless of where your spouse now lives, you must file your divorce complaint in Somerset County.)

- **If both you and your spouse were living outside of New Jersey at the time that your cause of action for divorce arose and you still live outside of New Jersey but your spouse now lives in New Jersey.** You must file your complaint in the New Jersey county where your spouse now lives. (For example, if you and your spouse were both living in Connecticut at the time that your cause of action for divorce arose, and you still live in Connecticut but your spouse now lives in Somerset County, New Jersey, you must file your divorce complaint in Somerset County.)

Filing Fee/Fee Waiver

You must pay a filing fee when you file the complaint. The filing fee is the court's charge for the services involved in processing the complaint. As of the time of publication of this manual, the filing fee for a divorce complaint is $250. If you have minor children, you must pay an additional $25 for a Parents' Education Program, which you are required to attend. The check must be made payable to *Clerk, Superior Court*. Check with your local county clerk's office for updated information on filing fees. (See Appendix A on page 112.)

If you cannot afford to pay the filing fee or the parent education fee, you may ask the court to waive these fees. To do so, you must file the following documents with your complaint:

- *Request for Waiver of Fees and Supporting Certification* **(Form 4).** This document explains your financial situation. You must sign the document, swearing that the statements are true.
- *Order Waiving Fees* **(Form 5).** This order states that you will not be required to submit a fee for filing. If the judge agrees with you, he or she will sign your proposed order and return a signed and filed copy of the order to you with a copy of your filed complaint.

After Your Complaint Is Filed

- **The filed copy.** The court will send you back a copy of your complaint with a stamp on it that says "filed." This copy will also have the name of the court, the date the complaint was filed, and a docket number for your case beginning with the letters "FM" (see below). If you have any questions about whether or not your document has been filed, check with the clerk's office at the county courthouse in the county named on the document.

  When you receive your filed copy, be sure to make at least three photocopies of it. You will need these copies for serving the defendant and for your records.

- **Docket number.** Once a docket number is given by the court, it is permanently assigned to your case. You must type or write this docket number on all of the papers you prepare that are related to the divorce action, including any letters you send out.

- **The judge in your case.** Usually, the Family Part or Dissolution Unit of the Superior Court will send you a notice telling you which judge will handle your case. If you do not receive this notice, you may call the court to find where your case has been assigned.

Checklist and Table of Documents for Filing the Complaint— Forms 1 through 6

Review your documents and package for the court to make sure that:

❑ You have filled in all the blanks in your complaint and in the other documents that you are sending to the court.

❑ Every document is signed and dated.

❑ You have enclosed a check for the filing fee and, if you and your spouse have children, the fee for the Parents' Education Program, if you are not asking for a waiver of the filing fees (**Forms 4** and **5**).

❑ You have asked for everything you want the court to grant.

❑ You are sending an original and two copies of all documents to the court.

❑ You have prepared and enclosed a self-addressed, stamped envelope (an envelope with your name, address, and postage on it) for the court to use to return filed copies to you.

❑ You have the right amount of postage on your package. We suggest that you have your package weighed and stamped at the post office. The court will not accept mail with inadequate postage.

❑ You have kept at least one extra copy of all documents for your records.

Forms for Chapter 1: Preparing and Filing the Divorce Complaint
Forms 1 through 6

Form #	Title of Form	Instructions
1A, IB, 1C, or 1D	Complaint for Divorce and Attached Certification	Send original and two copies to court clerk for filing.
2	Certification of Insurance	Attach to complaint or answer and counterclaim. Send original and two copies to court clerk for filing.
2A	Explanation of Dispute Resolution Alternatives	Read this explanation before filling out and signing Form 2B. This form *should not* be filed with the court.
2B	Certification of Notification of Complementary Dispute Resolution	Read Form 2A before filling out this certification. Attach to complaint or answer and counterclaim. Send original and two copies to clerk for filing.
3A	Family Part Case Information Statement (CIS)	File with complaint in cases where there is any issue about custody, support, alimony, or equitable distribution. Make sure copies of pay stubs, tax returns, and other required documents are attached.
3B	Confidential Litigant Information Sheet (CLIS)	DO NOT attach to the complaint or any other document that you file with the court. This is a confidential document for use by court personnel only.
4 and 5, if applicable	Request for Waiver of Fees and Supporting Certification, and Order Waiving Fees	Send original and two copies to court clerk for filing.
6	Filing Letter to Court— Complaint	Submit to court with Forms 1-5 for filing. Keep a copy for your records.

Chapter 2:
Serving the Divorce Complaint

This chapter will explain how to:
- Serve the defendant with the complaint and a summons.
- Pay service fees or other costs in order to serve the defendant.
- Give the court proof that the defendant was served.
- Keep track of time limits and deadlines.

This chapter will cover Forms 7 through 12B.

Chapter 2:
Serving the Divorce Complaint

If you are the plaintiff, you must make sure that the defendant is given a copy of the divorce complaint. This is called "serving" the defendant, and court rules require that service (the act of serving an individual) be done in a specific way. Court rules also require you to provide the court with proof that the defendant was served with the complaint in the way required by the rules.

Serve the complaint as soon as possible after the complaint has been returned from the court marked filed. The court can dismiss your case if you do not serve the defendant within four months of filing the complaint or if you do not inform the court about the reasons you have been unable to serve the defendant. We recommend that you send the defendant a photocopy of the complaint marked filed so it is clear to the defendant when the complaint was filed.

Serving the complaint is very important and, depending on the circumstances, can be complicated. From this point on, both the plaintiff and the defendant will need to keep track of time deadlines.

Preparing a Summons

You must serve the complaint with a *Summons and Attached Proof of Service* **(Form 7)**. The summons informs the defendant that he or she is being sued and must respond to the complaint within a specific period of time. The first thing that you must do is fill out the *Summons and Attached Proof of Service* **(Form 7)**. Follow the instructions for filling in all of the blanks. If you do not complete the form accurately and thoroughly, the court might find that you have not properly served the defendant, and you will have to attempt to serve the defendant all over again. This could be time-consuming and expensive for you.

At the end of the summons, a space is provided for you to fill in a description of the defendant. Provide the following information on the summons to make it easier for the sheriff to identify the defendant:
- A description of the defendant's physical appearance (height, weight, race).
- Special ways of identifying the defendant, such as hair and eye color, a beard or mustache, tattoos, birthmarks, or scars.
- If possible, the best times to find the defendant at home.

See *Summons and Attached Proof of Service* **(Form 7)** and *Cover Letter to Sheriff* **(Form 7A)**.

If you haven't already made photocopies of the filed copy of your complaint, make at least three photocopies now. You will need two copies for service, and you should keep at least one copy in your file.

Serving the Defendant

How you serve the defendant depends on whether you know his or her address and, if you do, whether he or she lives in New Jersey. It is usually easier to serve a defendant who lives in New Jersey and whose address is known.

Personal service is considered the best form of service and should be done by the sheriff's office. If the defendant does not have an attorney but is willing to cooperate with service, you may serve the defendant by mail. If the defendant has an attorney, you may serve the defendant by mail through his or her attorney.

If you cannot serve the defendant in person or by mail because you do not know where he or she lives, you will need to get permission from the court to serve the defendant another way, such as by serving another person who will probably be in touch with the defendant or by publishing a notice in a newspaper. This procedure is complicated and will require a lot of work on your part. It will also involve costs for mailing, including certified mail with return receipts and, possibly, costs for publication in a newspaper. You may want to consult an attorney to help you serve a defendant whose address is unknown to you. See page 49.

Note to victims of domestic violence: If you are hiding from your spouse because you are afraid and you have filed a complaint that does not contain your address and phone number, you will need to provide a post office box number or an alternative address where you can receive mail. To ensure your safety, you should consider obtaining an alternative address through the New Jersey Address Confidentiality Program (see page 21). You should also make sure to provide the post office box or alternative address on all correspondence to the defendant or to others to whom you may write in order to find the defendant for the purposes of serving him or her.

This chapter will explain how to serve a defendant in the following five situations:

> **A. Personal service on a New Jersey resident.** The defendant lives in New Jersey and can be served in person because you know his or her address. If this describes your situation, please turn to page 42 for instructions.

> **B. Personal service on an out-of-state defendant or a defendant in a foreign country.** The defendant lives in another state or in a foreign country, but can be served in person because you know his or her address. If this describes your situation, turn to page 44 for instructions.

C. Service by mail on a cooperative defendant. The defendant is cooperative and will agree to accept service by mail (the defendant can live in New Jersey or another state or in a foreign country). The defendant must sign a form called an acknowledgment of service in front of a notary and return the notarized form to you. If this describes your situation, turn to page 46 for instructions.

D. Service by mail on a cooperative defendant through the defendant's attorney. The defendant is cooperative and has an attorney who will agree to accept service by mail for the defendant (the defendant can live in New Jersey or another state or in a foreign country). If this describes your situation, turn to page 48 for instructions.

E. Service on a defendant whose address is unknown. You do not know where the defendant lives and, therefore, cannot serve the defendant in person. If this is your situation, please turn to page 49 for instructions.

A. Personal Service on a New Jersey Resident

The defendant lives in New Jersey and you know his or her address. The most reliable way to serve the defendant is to have a sheriff's officer in the county where the defendant lives serve him or her in person. If you have an order waiving fees, you should not have to pay the sheriff for serving the defendant. If you do not have a court order waiving fees, you will have to pay service and mileage fees to the sheriff. Call the sheriff's office to find out how much it will cost to pay the fees and mileage. Be aware, too, that you may have to pay additional fees if a sheriff's officer has to make several trips to serve a defendant.

Sending Documents to the Sheriff

You must mail or give the following documents to the sheriff of the county where the defendant lives. (See Appendix B on page 114 for a list of county sheriffs' offices.) Remember to keep a copy of each form for yourself.

- A *Cover Letter to Sheriff* (**Form 7A**).
- Two copies of the completed *Summons and Attached Proof of Service* (**Form 7**).
- Two copies of the *Complaint for Divorce* (**Form 1A, 1B, 1C, or 1D**) *and Attached Certification, Certification of Insurance* (**Form 2**), and *Certification of Notification of Complementary Dispute Resolution* (**Form 2B**), all marked filed.

- A check or money order for the service fee. (There is a fee for this service. To find out what the fee is, contact the sheriff's office. If you received permission from the court to file your divorce papers without paying the filing fee, include a signed copy of that order with your letter to the sheriff, and the sheriff's fees should be waived.)
- A self-addressed, stamped envelope so the sheriff can send the proof of service back to you once the defendant has been served.

Time Limits

On your calendar, note the date you sent the summons and complaint to the county sheriff's office, and make a note to call the sheriff's office two weeks from that date if you have not heard from that office.

Below is an explanation of what should happen once the sheriff's office receives your documents and check.

- **A sheriff's officer will serve the defendant.** A sheriff's officer will give the documents you sent to the defendant personally or will leave the documents at the defendant's home with any competent household member who is 14 years of age or older.
- **The sheriff's officer will sign a proof of service and send it to you in the self-addressed, stamped envelope that you have provided.** After

serving the defendant, the sheriff's officer will sign the proof of service on page 3 of the ***Summons and Attached Proof of Service*** (**Form 7**). The signed proof of service shows the defendant's name and the place, manner, and date of service. The date of service is important because the defendant has 35 days from the date that he or she is served to answer or respond in some way to the complaint for divorce. So, mark the date of service on your calendar and note when 35 days from that date is up. You may have to file more papers on that date, depending on what the defendant does after he or she is served.

Filing the Sheriff's Proof of Service

The sheriff's proof of service must be filed with the court where the divorce complaint is filed. The sheriff's officer is supposed to file the proof of service with the court and send you a copy. However, the sheriff's officer may not always remember to do that. You should file it yourself to make sure the court has it. Remember to keep a copy for yourself. If you do not get the sheriff's proof of service within 30 days of mailing the papers to the county sheriff's office, call that office to make sure you get it.

To file the sheriff's proof of service, send it to the clerk of the court with a ***Filing Letter to Court—Sheriff's Proof of Service*** (**Form 7B**) in the county where you filed your complaint. Send an original and one copy, plus a self-addressed, stamped envelope so the court can return a filed copy to you.

B. Personal Service on an Out-of-State Defendant or a Defendant in a Foreign Country

The defendant lives in another state or outside of the United States and you know his or her address. You may need to get some legal advice in order to do this kind of service. It can be a very complicated procedure to personally serve a defendant who lives in a foreign country. We do not recommend that you try to personally serve a defendant in a foreign country unless you know whom you have to contact, what the procedures are for serving divorce papers, and that you can afford to pay for the service.

It is less complicated to personally serve a defendant who lives in another state. You can easily find out what you have to do to get divorce papers served by calling either the sheriff, police, county clerk, or other public office in the defendant's city or town. Usually, it is a county sheriff's office that does this. However, some states have other officials who do this kind of service. You will have to do some research on your own to find out who does this kind of service and how much it will cost you.

Also, even if you have a waiver so that you do not have to pay fees in New Jersey—see *Order Waiving Fees* **(Form 5)**—your waiver is good only for New Jersey. You will have to pay service and mileage fees for service in a state other than New Jersey. Follow the instructions you are given by those out-of-state officials.

Sending Documents to an Out-of-State Sheriff or Other Agency

To satisfy the New Jersey courts' service requirements, you must send the following documents for service to an out-of state-sheriff or official:

- A *Cover Letter to Sheriff* **(Form 7A)**.
- Two copies of the completed *Summons and Attached Proof of Service* **(Form 7)**.
- Two copies of the *Complaint for Divorce* **(Form 1A, 1B, 1C, or 1D)** *and Attached Certification*, *Certification of Insurance* **(Form 2)**, and *Certification of Notification of Complementary Dispute Resolution* **(Form 2B)**, all marked filed.
- A check or money order for the service and mileage fees.
- A self-addressed, stamped envelope so the sheriff can send you a proof of service.

Time Limits

On your calendar, mark the date you sent the summons and complaint to the out-of-state sheriff's office or other agency and make a note to call that office two weeks from that date, if necessary.

Once the sheriff or other official sends you the proof of service, mark the date the defendant was served and the date 35 days from that date. The defendant has 35 days to respond to the divorce complaint. What you will have to do next will depend on whether or not the defendant files papers of his or her own within this 35-day period.

Filing the Sheriff's or Other Agent's Proof of Service

Once the defendant is served, the sheriff or other government official will send a proof of service back to you. You must then file it with the court. Send the *Filing Letter to Court—Sheriff's Proof of Service* (**Form 7B**) to the court in the county where you filed your complaint. Send an original and one copy, plus a self-addressed, stamped envelope so that the court can return a filed copy to you. Remember to keep a copy for yourself.

C. Service by Mail on a Cooperative Defendant

This quick and inexpensive method of service is only effective if the defendant will accept service and fill out and sign the *Acknowledgment of Service* (Form 8) in the presence of a notary and return it to you. (Notaries usually can be found at banks and at real estate and law offices.)

If the defendant accepts service and sends back a signed and notarized acknowledgment of service, you will have to file the acknowledgment with the court. Sometimes a defendant will not return the acknowledgment of service, but will instead file an answer to your divorce complaint with the court. In this situation, the court will still consider the defendant to have been properly served. The steps you must take after the defendant files an answer are explained in *Chapter 3: After Serving the Divorce Complaint* on page 65.

Sending Documents to the Defendant

You must send the following documents to the defendant by both regular mail *and* certified mail, return receipt requested. (Remember to keep the signed return receipt with your records. This is important in proving that the defendant has been served, especially if the defendant becomes uncooperative and you have to ask the court for permission to use another form of service.)

- A *Cover Letter to Defendant or Defendant's Attorney—Acknowledgment of Service* (Form 8A) explaining that the defendant should sign the acknowledgment of service in front of a notary, return the original to you, and retain one copy for his or her records.
- Two copies of the completed *Summons and Attached Proof of Service* (Form 7).
- Two copies of the *Complaint for Divorce* (Form 1A, 1B, 1C, or 1D) *and Attached Certification*, *Certification of Insurance* (Form 2), and *Certification of Notification of Complementary Dispute Resolution* (Form 2B), all marked filed.
- An *Acknowledgment of Service* (Form 8). The defendant should sign the form in front of a notary and return the notarized form to you. The defendant should keep a copy for his or her files.
- A self-addressed, stamped envelope so that the defendant can return the signed and notarized acknowledgment of service to you.

Filing the Acknowledgment of Service

After you get the signed and notarized acknowledgment of service form back from the defendant, immediately file it with the court. Make two copies of the signed acknowledgment. File the original and one copy with the court and keep the additional copy for your files. To file the acknowledgment, send the following to the court clerk:

- *Filing Letter to Court—Acknowledgment of Service* (**Form 8B**). Request that a filed copy be returned to you.
- Original and one copy of the signed and notarized *Acknowledgment of Service* (**Form 8**).
- Self-addressed, stamped envelope so that the court can send you a filed copy.

Timekeeping After You Receive the Signed Acknowledgment of Service

Mark the date the defendant was served and the date 35 days from that date. The defendant has 35 days to respond to the divorce complaint. If the defendant does not respond, you will have to file additional papers once this 35-day period has expired. What you will have to file will depend on whether or not the defendant files some papers of his or her own and what types of papers the defendant files. Your next steps will be covered in *Chapter 3: After Serving the Complaint* on page 65.

What to Do if the Defendant Becomes Uncooperative and Does Not Return the Acknowledgment of Service

If the defendant does not return the acknowledgment of service to you within three weeks, call the defendant to ask him or her to return it right away. If it is clear that the defendant is no longer willing to cooperate with you, you should immediately serve the defendant through the sheriff's office in the county where the defendant resides. If you fail to serve the defendant by mail, personal service is the most reliable alternative. See *Personal Service on a New Jersey Resident* on page 42, and *Personal Service on an Out-of-State Defendant or a Defendant in a Foreign Country* on page 44.

If you do not show the court that you have served the defendant within four months of filing your complaint, the court may take steps to dismiss your complaint.

D. Service by Mail on a Cooperative Defendant Through the Defendant's Attorney

If the defendant has an attorney, the defendant can authorize the attorney to accept service for him or her. If the attorney accepts service, this is considered the same as giving the papers to the defendant in person. The attorney will accept service and return an acknowledgment of service to you. Remember to include a self-addressed, stamped envelope. If the defendant agrees to do this, you must send the attorney the following documents by regular mail:

- A *Cover Letter to Defendant or Defendant's Attorney—Acknowledgment of Service* (Form 8A).

- Two copies of the completed *Summons and Attached Proof of Service* (Form 7).

- Two copies of the *Complaint for Divorce* (Form 1A, 1B, 1C, or 1D) *and Attached Certification*, *Certification of Insurance* (Form 2), and *Certification of Notification of Complementary Dispute Resolution* (Form 2B), all marked filed.

- An *Acknowledgment of Service* (Form 8). The defendant's attorney will sign the form and return it to you. The defendant's attorney will keep a copy for his or her files.

Filing the Acknowledgment of Service

After you get the signed and notarized acknowledgment of service form back from the defendant's attorney, you must file it with the court. Make two copies. File the original and one copy with the court and keep the additional copy for your files. To file the acknowledgment of service form, send the following to the court clerk:

- *Filing Letter to Court—Acknowledgment of Service* (Form 8B). Check off the appropriate box and request that a filed copy be returned to you.

- Original and one copy of the signed *Acknowledgment of Service* (Form 8).

- Self-addressed, stamped envelope so that the court can send you a filed copy.

Timekeeping After You Receive the Signed Acknowledgment of Service

Mark the date the defendant was served and the date 35 days from that date. The defendant has 35 days to respond to the divorce complaint. If the defendant does not respond, you will have to file additional papers once this 35-day period has expired. What you will have to file will depend on whether or not the defendant files some papers of his or her own and on what types of papers the defendant files. Your next steps will be covered in *Chapter 3: After Serving the Complaint* on page 65.

E. Service on a Defendant
Whose Address Is Unknown

When you do not know where the defendant lives, you are required to make "diligent inquiries" of all people or agencies that may know where the defendant lives. If, after your diligent inquiries, you do not find an address for the defendant, you will have to ask the court for permission to let you use an alternative method to serve the defendant. The court will generally grant permission for you to use an alternative method to serve the defendant, as long as you can demonstrate that you made "diligent efforts" to locate the defendant.

The alternative methods for serving a defendant whose address you do not know are:

- Serving a defendant by way of "substituted service on a special agent"—serving another person, in place of the defendant, who is likely to be able to give the summons and complaint to the defendant (often a relative or close friend of the defendant); or
- Serving a defendant by way of "publication"—publishing a notice of the divorce complaint in a newspaper.

Both of these methods are complicated. If you end up in this situation, you may want to seek legal assistance. If you decide to handle this procedure yourself, you need to follow the steps below. You must also make sure to keep copies of all of the written inquiries that you send and all of the responses you receive to your inquiries.

Step 1: Making Diligent Inquiries

Use *Letters of Inquiry* (**Forms 9** through **9H**), described below, to make inquiries of people and agencies that may have an address for the defendant. You must keep copies of the letters you send and the responses you receive so that you can submit them to the court as evidence of your attempts to find the defendant.

Send letters to:

- Your spouse's family members, close friends, or past employers who might know his or her address. These letters must be sent by both regular *and* certified mail, return receipt requested. *Letter of Inquiry to Defendant's Friends, Family, or Employers* (**Form 9**).

- The Motor Vehicle Commission (MVC) in the state where your spouse last held a driver's license. This letter should be sent by regular mail only. *Note:* We provide information for New Jersey. If you need information from another state, you must contact that other state's department of motor vehicles and ask them for the form they want you to use. *Letter of Inquiry to MVC* (**Form 9A**).

- All branches of the U.S. Military. Send these letters by regular mail only. *Letters of Inquiry to Military* (**Forms 9C** through **9H**).
- The post office in your town or in the town where the defendant last resided. Send this letter by regular mail only. Call the post office and ask if there is a search fee. If there is, enclose that fee with your letter. *Letter of Inquiry to Postmaster* (**Form 9B**).

Be sure to:

- Fill in all of the blanks as indicated on the forms.
- Make two copies of each completed letter. Mail one copy and keep the other in your file for use when you complete your supporting certifications for an order permitting an alternative method of service.
- Send the *Letter of Inquiry to Defendant's Friends, Family, or Employers* (**Form 9**) by both regular mail *and* by certified mail, return receipt requested.
- Send the other *Letters of Inquiry* (**Forms 9A** through **9H**) by regular mail.
- Enclose a self-addressed, stamped envelope with each letter to encourage the recipient to write back to you.
- Attach the signed return receipts or replies to your file copy of the letter you sent to that person. You will need these letters, return receipts, and any responses you receive when you get to Step 2.

Time Limits. On your calendar, mark the date you mailed the letters and the date three weeks from then so you know when it is time to take your next steps.

If someone to whom you wrote does provide you with an address for the defendant, you may try to serve the defendant in person at that address. See *Personal Service on a New Jersey Resident* on page 42. If the address is not in New Jersey, follow the instructions for *Personal Service on an Out-of-State Defendant* on page 44. If service is successful, you will file the proof of service with the court and wait (for at least 35 days) for a response from the defendant.

However, if you do not get an address, or if you do get an address but are not able to serve the defendant through the sheriff's office or by mail, you must apply to the court for permission to serve the defendant by one of the alternate methods. To do this, follow the instructions outlined in Step 2 below.

Step 2: Preparing Court Papers When You Cannot Serve the Defendant After Diligent Inquiries

If you do not get an address for the defendant through your diligent inquiries, you will have to ask the court for an order to serve the defendant by either substituted service on a special agent or by publication.

Requesting Substituted Service on a Special Agent. If someone you know or someone you wrote to is in touch with the defendant and will give the divorce papers to him or her, you may apply to the court for permission to serve that person in place of the defendant. The person acting as special agent for service must be 18 years of age or older. To make that application to the court, you must fill out **Forms 10A** and **10B** and attach all documents as instructed below.

- *Request for Order Permitting Substituted Service on a Special Agent and Supporting Certification* **(Form 10A)**. The supporting certification provides the court with information about your efforts to find the defendant, including:
    - The name of each person to whom you wrote.
    - Their relationship to the defendant—family member, friend, employer, business associate, government agency, military agency.
    - The date the letter was sent.
    - The nature of any responses you received.
    - The date and results of any phone calls, Internet searches, or other methods you used to find the defendant.

  In addition, attach the following items to the *Supporting Certification* **(Form 10A)**:
    - A copy of each letter you sent **(Forms 9** through **9H)**, with the return receipts and any replies that you received.
    - Copies of the certificate of non-military service that you received from the military.

- *Order Permitting Substituted Service on a Special Agent* **(Form 10B)**. This form lets the court know the name and address of the person (special agent) to be served in place of the defendant. The person acting as special agent for service must be 18 years of age or older. Also indicate the relationship of this person to the defendant—for example, mother, aunt, sister—and why you believe that person will be able to give the papers to the defendant.

- *Filing Letter to Court—Request for Substituted Service* **(Form 10C)**. Send this letter to the filing clerk of the court along with the original and two copies of the *Request for Order Permitting Substituted Service on a Special Agent and Supporting Certification* **(Form 10A)** and the *Order Permitting Substituted Service on a Special Agent* **(Form 10B)**.

Requesting Service by Publication. If you do not know where the defendant is and do not know anyone who could be appointed for substituted service upon the defendant, you will need to apply to the court for permission to serve the defendant by publishing a notice in a newspaper that is circulated in the county where the complaint was filed. To do this, you will have to complete **Forms 11A** and **11B**.

- *Request for Order Permitting Service by Publication and Supporting Certification* **(Form 11A).** The supporting certification provides the court with information about your efforts to find the defendant. Remember to sign and date the certification. For each person, business, or agency you wrote to, provide the court with the information below:
  - The name of each person to whom you wrote.
  - Their relationship to the defendant—family member, friend, employer, business associate, government agency.
  - The date of each letter.
  - The nature of any responses you received.
  - The date and results of any phone calls, Internet searches, or other methods you used to find the defendant.

  Attach the following items to your certification as exhibits:
  - A copy of each letter you sent **(Forms 9** through **9H)**, with the return receipts and any replies that you received.
  - Copies of the certificate of non-military service that you received from the military.

- *Order Permitting Service by Publication* **(Form 11B).** In this order, you may suggest the name of a local newspaper and ask the court to let you publish your notice in that newspaper; but the court makes the final decision as to which newspaper will publish the notice.

Step 3: Filing the Court Papers

Filing Instructions for an Order Permitting Substituted Service on a Special Agent. Mail the original plus two copies of each of the following forms to the court, along with a self-addressed, stamped envelope:

- *Filing Letter to Court—Request for Substituted Service* **(Form 10C).**
- *Request for Order Permitting Substituted Service on a Special Agent and Supporting Certification* **(Form 10A)** with attached letters of inquiry and replies.
- *Order Permitting Substituted Service on a Special Agent* **(Form 10B).**
- If filing fees have not been waived, you will have to pay a filing fee. (Call the court for the fee amount. Currently, the fee is $30.)
- If your filing fees have been waived, you will have to provide a copy of your signed *Order Waiving Fees* **(Form 5).**

Filing Instructions for an Order Permitting Service by Publication. Mail the original plus two copies of each of the following forms to the court, along with a self-addressed, stamped envelope:

- *Filing Letter to Court—Request for Service by Publication* **(Form 11C).**
- *Request for Order Permitting Service by Publication and Supporting Certification* **(Form 11A)**, with attached letters of inquiry and replies.
- *Order Permitting Service by Publication* **(Form 11B).**

- If filing fees have not been waived, you will have to pay a filing fee. (Call the court for the fee amount. Currently, the fee is $30.)

- If your filing fees have been waived, you will have to provide a copy of your signed *Order Waiving Fees* **(Form 5)**.

Time Limits. Mark the date you sent the papers to the court. If you do not receive the order within three weeks, call the court to find out whether it has been signed and when you will get it.

Step 4: Serving the Defendant

After you receive a copy of the signed order from the court allowing you to serve the defendant by substituted service on a special agent or by publication, you may proceed to serve the defendant.

Substituted Service on a Special Agent. If the court grants your request for substituted service, the judge will sign the *Order Permitting Substituted Service on a Special Agent* **(Form 10B)** and will name the special agent for service, usually the person you suggested in your certification. The judge will also specify in the order how that person is to be served. Usually, the order will state that the person is to be served personally through the sheriff's office. In this case, follow the instructions for *Personal Service on a New Jersey Resident* on page 42 or *Personal Service on an Out-of-State Defendant* on page 44. The order may also contain instructions for you to serve the person by registered or certified mail.

For service on a special agent, send the following documents to the sheriff or other government agent by regular *and* certified mail, return receipt requested:

- A *Cover Letter to Sheriff* **(Form 7A)**.
- Two copies of the completed *Summons and Attached Proof of Service* **(Form 7)**.
- Two copies of the *Complaint for Divorce* **(Form 1A, 1B, 1C, or 1D)** *and Attached Certification*, *Certification of Insurance* **(Form 2)**, and *Certification of Notification of Complementary Dispute Resolution* **(Form 2B)**, all marked filed.
- A copy of the *Order Permitting Substituted Service on a Special Agent* **(Form 10B)**.
- A check or money order for the service fee. (To find out what the fee is, contact the sheriff's office.) If you received permission from the court to file your divorce papers without paying the filing fee, include that signed *Order Waiving Fees* **(Form 5)** with your letter to the sheriff and the sheriff's fees should be waived if the service is being done in New Jersey.

- A self-addressed, stamped envelope.

Service by Publication. The signed *Order Permitting Service by Publication* **(Form 11B)** will tell you where to publish the notice of your divorce. You will have to prepare a *Notice of Order of Publication* **(Form 12)** to send to the newspaper. The notice contains information similar to that found in the *Summons and Attached Proof of Service* **(Form 7)**.

You must publish the *Notice of Order of Publication* **(Form 12)** in the newspaper specified in the order by the deadline specified in the signed *Order Permitting Service by Publication* **(Form 11B)**. Send the notice to the newspaper as soon as you receive the signed order so that you can be sure that you are in compliance with the court order. You will need to call the newspaper specified in the order to find out how much it will cost to publish the notice and where you should send the notice.

You will need to send the following to the newspaper immediately:

- A *Cover Letter to Newspaper Requesting Publication* **(Form 12A)**. Ask them to send you proof of publication.
- The *Notice of Order of Publication* **(Form 12)**.
- The fee for publication, payable to the newspaper. This fee is required, even for those who do not have to pay court filing fees.
- A self-addressed, stamped envelope.

Time Limits. Mark off a week before the final date for publication and, if you can, check the paper to make sure that they publish the notice. Call the newspaper to make sure that the notice will be published within the time specified by the court.

The newspaper must send you proof that the notice was published. This proof can be in the form of an *affidavit* or a certification. Make sure that you get a copy of the notice and certification. If you do not receive anything within seven days after the last date for publication, call the paper immediately to find out what the status is.

Once you receive the affidavit or certification of publication and a copy of the published notice from the newspaper, you will file them with the court. Send the following to the clerk of the court:

- A *Filing Letter to Court Re: Certification of Publication* **(Form 12B)**.
- The original and one copy of the certification and notice sent to you by the newspaper.
- A self-addressed, stamped envelope for return of the filed copy.

Important Information About
Keeping Track of Time for Your Next Steps

No matter which form of service you are using, you must keep track of time. Note the following dates on your calendar:

- **Service by mail.** The date you sent papers to the sheriff, the defendant, his attorney, a special agent for service, or to a newspaper for publication. You should follow up with them if you get no response within three weeks of the date you sent the papers.

- **Personal service.** The date the sheriff served the defendant or a special agent for service and the date 35 days later, which is the deadline for the defendant to respond to your complaint.

- **Acknowledgment of service.** If the defendant or his or her attorney was served by mail using an acknowledgment of service, mark the date the acknowledgment was signed and the date 35 days later, which is the deadline for the defendant to respond to your complaint.

- **Service by publication.** The date the newspaper notice was published and the date set by the court for the defendant to respond. The date for a response will be found in the order for publication.

Remember: You must serve the defendant as quickly as possible once you file your complaint. If you do not serve the defendant within four months after the date on which you filed your complaint, the court may dismiss your complaint. Always keep at least one copy of all of the papers related to your case, including cover letters.

Once the time for the defendant to respond to your complaint has expired, you move on to the next step or steps, which are explained in Chapters 4 and 5.

Flow Chart 2:
Service of Summons and Complaint

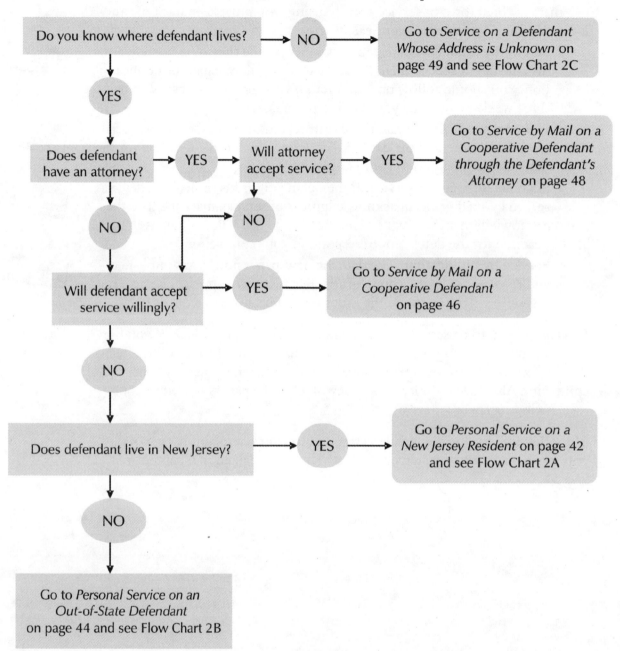

Flow Chart 2A:
Personal Service on a New Jersey Defendant

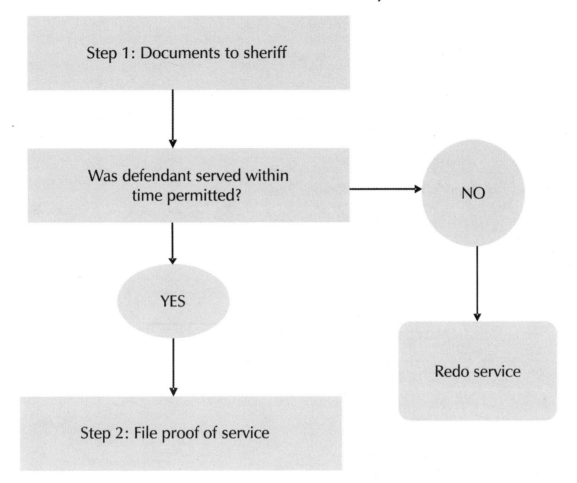

Flow Chart 2B:
Personal Service on an Out-of-State Defendant

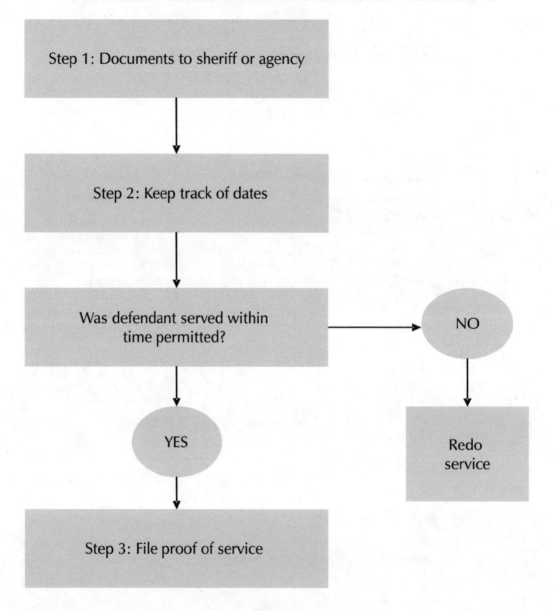

Flow Chart 2C:
Service on a Defendant Whose Address Is Unknown

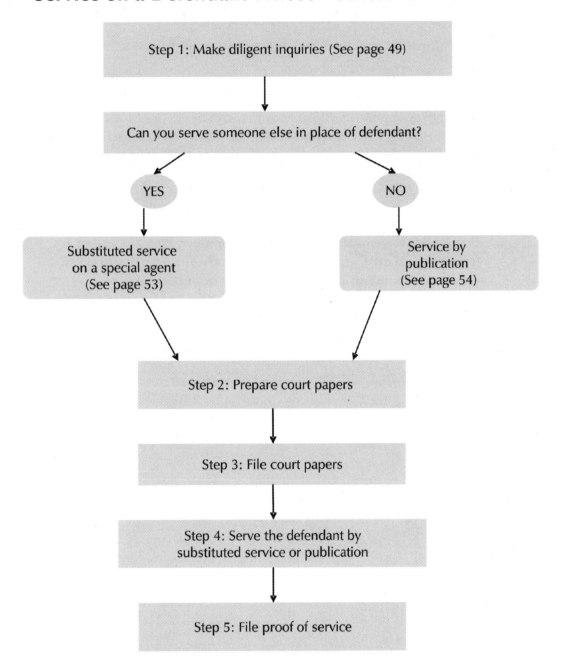

Step 1: Make diligent inquiries (See page 49)

Can you serve someone else in place of defendant?

YES

NO

Substituted service on a special agent (See page 53)

Service by publication (See page 54)

Step 2: Prepare court papers

Step 3: File court papers

Step 4: Serve the defendant by substituted service or publication

Step 5: File proof of service

Checklist and Table of Documents for Serving the Divorce Complaint— Forms 7 through 12B

❑ Don't forget to enclose a check or money order for the service fee.

❑ If your filing fees and service fees were waived when you filed your divorce complaint, send a copy of the signed order waiving fees to the New Jersey county sheriff's office that will be doing the service. (*Note:* New Jersey sheriff's officers should not charge for service if fees have been waived. However, most out-of-state sheriff's officers will charge service fees, regardless of your court order.)

❑ Send the proper service and mileage fees as required.

❑ Remember to include a self-addressed, stamped envelope when you write to the sheriff, courts, agencies, or individuals so that you can receive a response or the return of copies of important papers.

❑ Always keep at least one copy of every paper you send out.

❑ Attach return receipts to the copy of the appropriate letter.

Form #	Title of Form	Instructions
Forms for Chapter 2: Serving the Divorce Complaint **Forms 7 through 12B**		
Forms 7, 7A, and 7B—Personal Service on Defendant by Sheriff		
7 **7A**	Summons and Attached Proof of Service Cover Letter	Send original and two copies to sheriff's office with your complaint and all attached certifications. Keep a copy for your records. Sheriff will return proof of service when service is completed.
7B	Filing Letter to Court—Sheriff's Proof of Service	Submit to court clerk with original and two copies of completed Proof of Service (Form 7).
Forms 8, 8A, and 8B—Service by Mail on Cooperative Defendant		
8 **8A**	Acknowledgment of Service Cover Letter to Defendant or Defendant's Attorney	Send to defendant or defendant's attorney via regular *and* certified mail, return receipt requested. Enclose your complaint and all certifications. Keep a copy for your records.
8B	Filing Letter to Court—Acknowledgment of Service	Send original and two copies of signed and notarized Form 8 to court clerk for filing.
Forms 9 through 9H—Letters of Diligent Inquiry		
9	Letter of Inquiry to Defendant's Friends, Family, or Employers	Send original via regular *and* certified mail, return receipt requested. Keep a copy of each for your records.
9A	Letter of Inquiry to MVC	Same as for Form 9.
9B	Letter of Inquiry to Postmaster	Same as for Form 9.
9C	Letter of Inquiry to Military	Same as for Form 9.
9D	Letter of Inquiry to Military (Army)	Same as for Form 9.
9E	Letter of Inquiry to Military (Air Force)	Same as for Form 9.
9F	Letter of Inquiry to Military (Navy)	Same as for Form 9.
9G	Letter of Inquiry to Military (Marine Corps)	Same as for Form 9.
9H	Letter of Inquiry to Military (Coast Guard)	Same as for Form 9.

Forms 10A, 10B, and 10C—Substituted Service on Special Agent		
10A	Request for Order Permitting Substituted Service on a Special Agent and Supporting Certification	Send original and two copies to the court clerk for filing along with Form 10B. Attach copies of letters of inquiry (Forms 9-9H) and replies, if any, to supporting certification.
10B	Order Permitting Substituted Service on a Special Agent	Send original and two copies to the court clerk for filing along with Form 10A.
10C	Filing Letter to Court—Request for Substituted Service	Send to the court with Forms 10A and 10B. Keep a copy for your records.
Forms 11A through 12B—Service by Publication		
11A	Request for Order Permitting Service by Publication and Supporting Certification	Send original and two copies to the court for filing along with Form 11B. Attach copies of letters of inquiry (Forms 9-9H) and replies, if any, to supporting certification.
11B	Order Permitting Service by Publication	Send original and two copies to the court for filing along with Form 11A.
11C	Filing Letter to Court—Request for Service by Publication	Send to the court with Forms 11A and 11B. Keep a copy for your records.
12	Notice of Order of Publication	Send to newspaper after you receive signed order (Form 11B). Keep a copy for your records.
12A	Cover Letter to Newspaper Requesting Publication	Send to newspaper with Form 12. Keep a copy for your records.
12B	Filing Letter to Court Re: Certification of Publication	Send with an original and two copies of certification of publication from newspaper to the court for filing. Keep a copy for your records.

Chapter 3:
After Serving the Divorce Complaint

This chapter will explain:

- How long a defendant has to respond to the complaint.
- What is contained in a defendant's answer, or answer and counter-claim, and how to file and serve this document.
- What information is contained in plaintiff's answer to counterclaim and how to file and serve this.

This chapter will cover Forms 13 through 16.

Chapter 3:
After Serving the Divorce Complaint

What happens next in your case will depend on whether the defendant answers your complaint. We instructed you to mark on your calendar both the date the defendant was served and 35 days after that date. (See *Chapter 2: Serving the Divorce Complaint* on page 39.) Usually, the defendant's answer is due 35 days after service. However, if the defendant was served by substituted service or by publication, the court may have given the defendant a longer time period to answer.

Time Frames for the Defendant

If the defendant wants to contest your claims or participate in this case, the defendant must answer the complaint as follows:

- **If the complaint was personally served by the sheriff.** The defendant must file an answer to the divorce complaint or some other type of written response within 35 days of receiving the complaint.

- **If the defendant or his or her attorney signed an acknowledgment of service.** The defendant must file an answer or enter an appearance within 35 days of signing the acknowledgment of service.

- **If the defendant was served by substituted service or by publication.** The defendant has to answer or enter an appearance by the date specified on the order permitting either substituted service or publication.

The defendant can ask for an extension of time so that he or she can file an answer. See *Consent Order Extending Time to Answer* (Form 13). You may consent to giving the defendant up to a 60-day extension of time to answer, but you cannot agree to extend the time beyond 60 days without permission of the court. You and the defendant must both sign a consent order if you agree to an extension. The defendant must file the consent order with the court before the time to answer the complaint is up. See *Filing Letter to Court—Consent Order Extending Time to Answer* (Form 13A). If you do not agree, or if the defendant wants to get an extension beyond 60 days, the defendant will have to file a motion asking the court for permission.

Defendant Does Not Respond to the Complaint

If the defendant does not answer the complaint or obtain an extension of time to answer the complaint, you can ask the court for what is called a *default judgment* in your case. If this is your situation, go directly to *Chapter 4: Getting a Default Judgment* on page 75. There are still papers to prepare and a few things that you will have to do, but the good news is that, at this point, you are very close to getting your divorce.

Defendant Responds to the Complaint— Forms for Defendants

Defendant's Appearance

Sometimes a defendant, in response to receiving a complaint for divorce, will enter a general appearance. If this happens, the plaintiff may receive a document called a "general appearance" or an acknowledgment of service. (See page 46.) When the defendant files one of these documents, it puts you and the court on notice that the defendant is not contesting the allegations of the divorce and is not requesting a divorce, but is reserving the right to contest some or all of the relief that you asked for, such as child support, spousal support, child custody, parenting time/visitation, and equitable distribution. The defendant can also contest the relief in a counterclaim filed with an answer. (See below.)

Defendant's Answer

In his or her answer, the defendant admits the allegations that are true and denies those claims that are false. If the defendant wants to file allegations against you, he or she must do this when answering the complaint. The defendant's allegations against you are written in what is called a *counterclaim* for divorce, which is filed with the answer. Sometimes a defendant will file only an answer without a counterclaim. In this manual, we do not provide a form for an answer without a counterclaim. *If the defendant files only an answer without a counterclaim within 35 days,* there is nothing else that you must file. For an explanation of what to do in this situation, go directly to *Chapter 5: Going to Court When the Defendant Is Not in Default—Contested and Uncontested Cases* on page 87.

Defendant's Counterclaim

If the defendant decides to file a counterclaim, he or she will file a form that is similar in format to a complaint, except that it is filed from the point of view of the defendant and offers his or her reasons for divorce. The defendant can base his or her counterclaim on the same grounds for divorce or on different grounds. The defendant may set forth any requests for relief he or she wants to make, including custody, support, name change, tort claims, and division of property and debt. See the items below:

- Filing fee (call the court clerk for filing fee information).
- *Answer and Counterclaim for Divorce Based on Separation and Attached Certification* (Form 14A).
- *Answer and Counterclaim for Divorce Based on Desertion and Attached Certification* (Form 14B).
- *Answer and Counterclaim for Divorce Based on Extreme Cruelty and Attached Certification* (Form 14C).
- *Answer and Counterclaim for Divorce Based on Irreconcilable Differences and Attached Certification* (Form 14D).

Other Documents to Be Filed by Defendant With the Answer and Counterclaim

Make four photocopies of every document you prepare. You will send the original and two copies to the court and keep the extra two copies for your records and for later use. The docket number assigned to the case when the complaint was filed must appear on all of the documents that you file in the case.

Always include a self-addressed, stamped envelope (an envelope that has both postage and your name and address on it) with any documents that you send to the court so that the court can send you back a copy marked filed. You should do this even if you hand-deliver your papers to the court. You may need to know the date on which the court received something, and the filed document will have the date, time, and location of the filing on it.

There are other documents that must be filed with an answer and counterclaim. They are explained in detail below. Please look at the forms as you read the instructions.

Other forms the defendant must file with the answer and counterclaim include:

- *Filing Letter to Court—Answer and Counterclaim for Divorce* (Form 14E). Your filing letter lets the court know what you are sending and requests a filed copy of the answer and counterclaim. The filing letter also indicates whether you are paying the filing fee or seeking a fee waiver (which will only be given if you truly cannot afford the filing fee), as explained on page 33. Make sure to check off all appropriate boxes.
- *Certification of Verification and Non-Collusion* (attached to the answer and counterclaim). This is a sworn statement that appears at the end of your answer and counterclaim (**Form 14A, 14B, 14C, or 14D**). It lets the court know that:
  - All of the claims and facts in the answer and counterclaim are true.
  - There is no other divorce action, or any other legal matter involving you or your spouse, presently filed in any court or arbitration proceeding. (If there is some other legal matter involving you and your spouse, you must let the court know what it is.)
  - There are no other people who should be included in this divorce.

  You have a continuing obligation to update this information if it changes during the time that the divorce is pending in court. If the information is untrue or is not updated, the court may dismiss your answer and counterclaim.
- *Certification of Insurance* (Form 2). This is a separate form that must be attached to your answer and counterclaim. It lists all known insurance coverage for you, your spouse, and your minor children. This includes life, health, automobile, and homeowners insurance. Any insurance

coverage identified in the certification of insurance at the time the answer and counterclaim is filed must be maintained until the court orders otherwise. If you do not file this document with your answer and counterclaim, the clerk may refuse to file your answer and counterclaim.

- **Certification of Notification of Complementary Dispute Resolution (Form 2B)**. This is another form that must be attached to your answer and counterclaim. It states that you have been informed about dispute resolution alternatives that you may use to settle your case. Before you sign this document, you must read the information contained in the **Explanation of Dispute Resolution Alternatives (Form 2A)**.

- **Family Part Case Information Statement (CIS) (Form 3A).** This must be filed with your answer and counterclaim if there is an issue of custody, support, alimony, or division of property and debt (equitable distribution). Even if you are not seeking these types of relief, the court may require you to complete a CIS. The CIS asks for detailed information about the financial circumstances, income, and assets of each party. The financial papers you gathered during your planning will help you give accurate information to the court about your financial circumstances. You will also have to photocopy and attach some financial documents to this form, such as tax returns and pay stubs. See the instructions on this form. It is important that this information be accurate and true.

- **Confidential Litigant Information Sheet (CLIS) (Form 3B)**. If you are requesting alimony or child support as relief, the court requires you to fill out and file this form at the same time that you file your answer and counterclaim . The purpose of the CLIS is to provide the court with relevant updated personal information to be used only for the purposes of establishing and modifying and enforcing orders for child support or spousal support. This form will be used to update the official state computer system with information to assist the court in contacting you when necessary. The CLIS is a confidential document. This means that the information in the CLIS may not be shared with any member of the public. For that reason, it should not be attached to the complaint or any other document filed with the court. This is because, once a complaint or other document is filed with the court, it is considered to be a public record and is accessible by any member of the public.

  Note to victims of domestic violence: To ensure your safety, if you are hiding from your spouse, you should consider obtaining an alternative address through the New Jersey Address Confidentiality Program (see page 21).

- **Request for Waiver of Fees and Supporting Certification (Form 4)** and **Order Waiving Fees (Form 5)**. If you cannot afford the filing fees, file **Forms 4** and **5** to get permission from the court to waive the fees. (This is explained under *Filing Fee/Fee Waiver* on page 33.) If you can afford the fees for filing and, if you and your spouse have children, for the Parents' Education Program, you will simply pay the fees by check when you file your papers. Call the court clerk to find out the amount of these fees. (See Appendix A on page 112 for the phone numbers of court clerks.)

- **A self-addressed, stamped envelope.** On the front of your package to the court, enclose an envelope containing postage and your name and address so the court can return a filed copy of the papers to you. It is very important that you have copies of your documents marked filed. You will need them for your records and for later use. The court will not send you these filed copies unless you provide the self-addressed, stamped envelope.

- *Certification of Service* **(Form 16)**. This is filed with the answer or answer and counterclaim instead of a summons to prove to the court that you have properly served this document on the other party.

How to Answer the Defendant's Counterclaim— Forms for Plaintiffs

You answer the defendant's counterclaim by filing an *Answer to Counterclaim for Divorce* **(Form 15A),** admitting or denying the allegations that the defendant made in his or her counterclaim against you. You must admit or deny the allegations of every paragraph of the counterclaim. Our form indicates where you add the word "admit" or "deny" and provides space to answer a counterclaim that contains as many as four counts or grounds for divorce. The *Certification of Service* **(Form 16)** is filed with the *Answer to Counterclaim for Divorce* **(Form 15A)** to prove that you have properly served this document on the other party. You must send your *Answer to Counterclaim for Divorce* **(Form 15A)** and *Certification of Service* **(Form 16)** to the defendant and to the court as follows:

- To the defendant or his or her attorney:
  - If the defendant has an attorney, send by regular mail to the attorney.
  - If the defendant is *pro se* (representing him- or herself), mail to the defendant by both regular *and* certified mail, return receipt requested.

- To the court for filing, use:
  - *Answer to Counterclaim for Divorce* **(Form 15A)** and *Certification of Service* **(Form 16)**.
  - *Filing Letter to Court—Answer to Counterclaim for Divorce* **(Form 15B)**.
  - A self-addressed, stamped envelope so that the court will return a filed copy to you.

Checklist for Filing Documents and Table of Documents— Forms 13 through 16

Review your documents and package for the court to make sure that:

❑ You have filled in all the blanks on your answer and counterclaim and other documents that you are sending to the court.

❑ Every document is signed and dated.

❑ If you are filing an answer or an answer and counterclaim, you have enclosed a check for the filing fee if you are not asking for a waiver of the filing fees (**Forms 4** and **5**).

❑ You are sending an original and two copies of all documents to the court.

❑ You have prepared and enclosed a self-addressed, stamped envelope (an envelope with your name, address, and postage on it) for the court to use to return filed copies to you.

❑ You have the right amount of postage on your package. We suggest that you have your package weighed and stamped at the post office. The court will not accept mail with inadequate postage.

❑ You have kept at least one extra copy of all documents for your records.

❑ You have marked on your calendar:

   o The dates you sent your documents to the court.
   o The date 10 days from the date you sent your documents with a note to call the court clerk if you have not received your filed copy of the documents back from the court.

Forms for Chapter 3: After Serving the Divorce Complaint
Forms 13 through 16

Form #	Title of Form	Instructions
Documents to Be Filed by a Defendant—Forms 4 & 5 and Forms 13 through 14E		
4 and 5, if applicable	Request for Waiver of Fees and Supporting Certification, and Order Waiving Fees	Send original and two copies to court clerk for filing.
13	Consent Order Extending Time to Answer	Send original and two copies to court clerk for filing.
13A	Filing Letter to Court—Consent Order Extending Time to Answer	Send to court clerk with Form 13.
14A, 14B, 14C, or 14D	Answer and Counterclaim for Divorce and Attached Certification	Send original and two copies to court clerk for filing, along with Forms 2 and 2B. **In cases where there is any issue as to custody, support, alimony, or equitable distribution,** send Forms 3A and 3B to court clerk for filing within 20 days after filing answer.
14E	Filing Letter to Court—Answer and Counterclaim for Divorce	Send to court clerk with Form 14A, 14B, 14C, or 14D, and Forms 2, 2B and 16.
Documents Plaintiff Files if Defendant Submits an Answer and Counterclaim to Divorce—Forms 15A through 16		
15A	Answer to Counterclaim for Divorce	Send original and two copies to court clerk for filing along with Form 16.
15B	Filing Letter to Court—Answer to Counterclaim for Divorce	Send with Forms 15A and 16.
16	Certification of Service	Send with specific designated forms (see above and below).

Chapter 4:
Getting a Default Judgment

This chapter will provide step-by-step instructions for getting a divorce judgment against a defendant who does not file a written answer to your complaint.

This chapter will cover Forms 17 through 21A.

Chapter 4:
Getting a Default Judgment

If you served the defendant properly and the defendant does not file a written response (answer, acknowledgment of service, counterclaim) to the complaint within the time allowed (35 days from the date of service, unless the court has allowed an extension of time or provided a specific time period in an order for alternate service), you may ask the court for a default judgment in your favor. This means that a judge will sign an order deciding the issues in the case without the defendant's participation.

The default judgment does not happen automatically. The procedure requires several steps. The steps that you must follow to request a default judgment are listed below, along with a brief explanation of the forms that you will have to fill out and file.

Procedure to Obtain the Entry of a Default Judgment and a Default Divorce Hearing

File a Request for a Default

When the defendant's time to answer the complaint has expired (that is, more than 35 days have passed since the date the defendant was served, or the period of time provided in the order for alternative service has expired), call the court clerk to make sure that no answer has been filed in your divorce action. Once that is confirmed, you must prepare the following documents and file them with the court:

MARK THIS DATE

- *Request to Enter Default Judgment and Supporting Certification* **(Form 17).**
- *Certification of Non-Military Service* **(Form 18).**

Note: If you do not request a default within *six months* of the date that the defendant failed to respond to your complaint, you will have to file a motion with the court seeking permission to obtain a default judgment, costing you additional time and money. This manual does not explain that procedure.

Mail an original and one copy of the following to the court:
- *Filing Letter to Court—Request to Enter Default Judgment* **(Form 17A).**
- *Request to Enter Default Judgment and Supporting Certification* **(Form 17).** In response to this request, you should get a date for your hearing from the court.
- *Certification of Non-Military Service* **(Form 18).** You cannot get a default judgment against your spouse if he or she is in the military. In applying for the entry of a default judgment, the court requires the plaintiff to submit a sworn statement that the defendant is not in military service.

If you have personal knowledge that the defendant is not in the military, you may fill out and sign a ***Certification of Non-Military Service* (Form 18)**. Personal knowledge means that you are relying on your own firsthand knowledge, not something that your spouse or someone else has told you. If you do not have personal knowledge, you must base your statement on the written responses from the branches of the military that you receive in response to your inquiries.

To obtain a statement from the Department of Defense (DOD), you must know the defendant's Social Security number. If you do not have this information, you may not be able to get the statement that you need from the DOD. Instead, you should contact the specific branch of the military. However, if you *do not know* what branch of the military to contact, a statement from the Department of Defense (DOD) that the defendant is not in the military may substitute for a statement or certificate from a specific branch of the military government. The DOD Web site is ***www.defenselink.mil***. Or you can mail a letter to the Defense Manpower Data Center of the DOD. (See ***Letter of Inquiry to the Military (DOD)* (Form 9C)**). There is no charge for this statement.

When you *do know* which branch of the military to contact, you may contact the specific branch of the military (Army, Air Force, Navy, Marine Corps, Coast Guard) by visiting ***https://www.dmdc.osd.mil/scra/owa/home***. The Web site contains additional information. You must then mail a letter to the appropriate branch of the military. (See ***Letters of Inquiry to the Military [Army, Air Force, Navy, Marine Corps, Coast Guard]* (Forms 9D** through **9H)**). For the Marine Corps only, mark the bottom of the envelope *Official Business*. The locator service is free to immediate family members and government officials. All others must pay $5.20. Checks or money orders should be made payable to the agency listed in the letter of inquiry.

If You Are Unable to Get a Statement About the Defendant's Military Status. If you do not have firsthand knowledge about whether or not the defendant is in military service and you are unable to get an official statement from the DOD or another branch of the military about whether or not the defendant is serving in the military, you must report this to the court. Without this information, you cannot file the required ***Certification of Non-Military Service* (Form 18)** with the court at the time that you request the entry of default judgment.

In situations where you are unable to get any definite information or official statement about the defendant's military status, the court may feel that it is necessary to require that you post a bond (pay a certain sum of money into the court) to protect the defendant's rights. The reason for requiring you to set aside money is to pay the defendant for any loss or damage that he or she might suffer as a result of not participating in the divorce through no fault of his own because of active duty in the military.

The bond money must be available until the time for the defendant to *appeal* from the judgment of divorce has ended. When a party appeals from a judgment, he or she files a notice of appeal to the Superior Court, Appellate Division, for a review of the trial court's decision. (You have 45 days from the date that the judgment is entered by the trial court to file an appeal.) The court may also require that the bond money be available until the time for setting aside the judgment of divorce has ended. (The time for setting aside a judgment can be a year or longer.)

This means that, in certain situations where the defendant stands to lose significant property through a divorce, the court may require you to post a bond. In those situations, if you cannot afford to post a bond, you may not be able to get your divorce. However, in a situation where there is no significant marital property that needs to be divided, the court may waive the requirement that you post a bond and allow the divorce action to go forward.

If You Are Able to Get a Statement About the Defendant's Military Status.
Attach the responses that you get to the *Certification of Non-Military Service* **(Form 18)**.

File **Form 18** with the *Certification of Service* **(Form 16)** and a self-addressed, stamped envelope so that a filed copy of your papers can be returned to you.

Send the Defendant a Copy of the Request to Enter Default

Send this by both regular *and* certified mail, return receipt requested, at the same time that you file it with the court. Save the return receipt, because you will need it later when you go to court for your default hearing.

Get a Date for Your Default Divorce Hearing

Mark your calendar to call the clerk two weeks after you send the request to enter default to get a date for your hearing. If you do not hear from the court within two weeks, call the clerk of the matrimonial department and inquire about the hearing date. (See telephone numbers and addresses in Appendix A on page 112.)

Send the Defendant a *Notice of Default Divorce Hearing*

When you receive the date for your hearing from the court, fill out the *Notice of Default Divorce Hearing* **(Form 19)** and mail it to the defendant by both regular *and* certified mail, return receipt requested. If you are *not* seeking custody, child support, or equitable distribution, you will send a copy of **Form 19** to the defendant with a *Cover Letter to Defendant—Notice of Default Divorce Hearing* **(Form 19A)**. You also should send a copy of the *Notice of Default Divorce Hearing* **(Form 19)** with a *Certification of Service* **(Form 16)** to the court. If you are seeking custody, support, or equitable distribution, you must take the additional steps below.

Additional Steps if You Are Seeking Custody, Child Support, Equitable Distribution, or Other Relief

If the defendant has not answered the complaint and you are asking for more than just a divorce and a name change—for example, you are asking for property or a division of debts, child support, or alimony—you will need to take some additional steps. You must:

- Prepare a *Notice of Application for Equitable Distribution* (Form 20) and a *Certification of Service* (Form 16).
- Prepare the *Filing Letter to Court—Notice of Application for Equitable Distribution* (Form 20A).
- File an original and one copy of the *Notice of Application for Equitable Distribution* (Form 20) and *Certification of Service* (Form 16) with the court.
- At the same time that you file the *Notice of Application for Equitable Distribution* (Form 20) with the court, mail it to the defendant by both regular *and* certified mail, return receipt requested.

Note that it is very important that the defendant be served with the notice *no later than 20 days before your hearing* and that you have the return receipts and certification of service when you go to court. If you do not serve the defendant with this notice 20 days or more before your hearing, the court will not consider your request for equitable distribution. You may get a divorce, but you may not get any money or property awarded to you and the judge may *not* order the defendant to pay alimony, child support, back debts, or any of the other things for which you are asking.

How to Prove to the Court that the Defendant Received the *Notice of Application for Equitable Distribution* Within 20 Days of the Date of the Default Hearing

At the default hearing, you will be required to show proof that the defendant either received or refused the notice of application for equitable distribution at least 20 days prior to the scheduled default hearing date. Proof that the defendant received the notice can include either the green return receipt card with a signature, or the envelope stamped by the post office "unclaimed" or "refused."

Note: An envelope returned and marked "incorrect address" or otherwise indicating that the correspondence is undeliverable is not valid proof that the defendant received or refused the notice of application for equitable distribution.

What to Do if the Defendant Does Not Receive the *Notice of Application for Equitable Distribution* Within 20 Days of the Date of the Default Hearing

If the date on the green return receipt card indicates that the notice of application for equitable distribution was delivered to the defendant less than

20 days before the default hearing, or if you do not know when the defendant received the notice of application for equitable distribution because you have not yet received proof of delivery or refusal from the post office and the default hearing is scheduled in two or three days, you will have to ask for a new date for the default hearing. To do this, you must contact the clerk of the matrimonial department or the judge's chambers. (See phone numbers and addresses in Appendix A on page 112.)

Tell the clerk that you attempted to serve the defendant with the notice of application for equitable distribution, but it was delivered too late; or that you do not know when the defendant received the notice of application for equitable distribution, because you have not yet received the proof of delivery from the post office. In either situation, ask the clerk for a new default hearing date, with at least 40 days advance notice (or as much time as you think that you will need to serve the defendant with a new notice of application for equitable distribution). See *Filing Letter to Court—Request to Enter Default Judgment* (Form 17A).

Once you have the new court date for the default hearing, you must send the defendant a new notice of application for equitable distribution with the new default hearing date. You can use the *Notice of Application for Equitable Distribution* (Form 20) and the *Notice of Default Divorce Hearing* (Form 19) for this purpose.

If there have been any changes in your financial circumstances, you are required to send in an updated *Family Part Case Information Statement (CIS)* (Form 3A). Also use the *Filing Letter to Court—Complaint* (Form 6), which is the cover letter you used when you filed your complaint.

Getting Ready for Your Default Divorce Hearing

Once you send out your request for default, it is a good time to review your file and put all of your divorce papers in order. This will help you to prepare for your hearing, and you may need some of these papers when you go to court. You should also prepare your proposed *Final Default Judgment of Divorce* (Form 21) to take with you to court on the day of your default hearing.

Here is a list of the divorce papers you should have with you in your file, just in case you need them or need to refer to them for some reason. We suggest that you put them in chronological order, so that the most recent document that you prepared—your proposed *Final Default Judgment of Divorce* (Form 21), which you will be bringing to court—is on top.

Papers Needed for Court—Your Case File

- The filed copy of your *Complaint for Divorce and Attached Certification* **(Form 1A, 1B, 1C, or 1D)**.
- *Certification of Insurance* **(Form 2)**.
- *Certification of Notification of Complementary Dispute Resolution* **(Form 2B)**.
- *Family Part Case Information Statement (CIS)* **(Form 3A)**.
- *Summons and Attached Proof of Service* **(Form 7)** and one or more of the following documents, depending on how the defendant was served:
  - If service was done through a sheriff, the sheriff's proof of service or, if the complaint was served on the defendant in another state, proof of service from an appropriate state official.
  - If service was done by mail, the signed and notarized *Acknowledgment of Service* **(Form 8)**.
  - If service was done by substituted service or publication:
    - ✓ Either *Order Permitting Substituted Service on a Special Agent* **(Form 10B)** or *Order Permitting Service by Publication* **(Form 11B)**.
    - ✓ Either return receipt from mailing to a special agent or proof of publication from the newspaper.
    - ✓ *Certification of Non-Military Service* **(Form 18)** and, if applicable, attached certificates of non-military service from each branch of the service that you wrote to in your diligent inquiries.
- *Notice of Application for Equitable Distribution* **(Form 20)** and *Certification of Service* **(Form 16)** with return receipt attached.
- *Notice of Default Hearing* **(Form 19)** and *Certification of Service* **(Form 16)**.
- Proposed *Final Default Judgment of Divorce* **(Form 21)**.

You should also have the following personal documents with you:
- Marriage certificate.
- Birth certificates for the children.

The Default Divorce Hearing

At the default divorce hearing, the court must address the requests for relief in your complaint. Often there are issues, such as the division of property or the calculation of alimony, that cannot be decided without some type of proof. In that situation, the judge will hold a hearing to decide what relief to grant. You may present evidence at the hearing supporting your requests for this relief.

The defendant can come to this hearing if he or she chooses, even if he or she did not answer the complaint. The defendant can ask for an adjournment (postponement) to give him or her time to answer the complaint. The court will most probably grant this request if the defendant gives a good explanation of why he or she failed to answer earlier in the process. In that case, the court will decide at that time when the defendant's answer is due. The court will either inform the plaintiff and defendant of the new hearing or trial date while both parties are in court on the day of the default hearing, or the court will send a notice to both parties with a new date for the hearing or trial. If the court decides to give the defendant an opportunity to file an answer, the court will also inform both parties of the date on which that answer is due to be filed.

Note: If the defendant files a counterclaim with his or her answer, refer to page 69 for an explanation of how to properly prepare and file an *Answer to Counterclaim for Divorce* (Form 15A).

If the defendant appears but does not ask for an adjournment and the default hearing goes on as scheduled, the court may limit the defendant's participation to asking you questions about the evidence you present. Technically, the defendant should not be given an opportunity to present evidence to support his or her position or to make requests for relief. However, some judges will let the defendant participate fully in the hearing and present his or her own evidence. You can object to this participation, remind the judge that the defendant failed to file an answer or enter an appearance in the case, and ask that the divorce be treated as uncontested.

At the hearing, you will be able to show evidence related to your claims about property value, child custody, child support, alimony, and other issues. The documents in your file should have everything you need for the hearing, including the return receipts for all of the documents you had to mail to the defendant and the responses you received to your letters of diligent inquiry, including the certificates of non-military service. You should also have copies of tax returns, pay stubs, bills, bank statements, real estate appraisals, etc.

Final Judgment of Divorce Where Defendant Is in Default

The court order that officially ends your marriage is called a *final judgment of divorce.* You should prepare that order and take it to your hearing. That court order decides all of the issues that you have raised in your divorce complaint, such as custody, child support, alimony, equitable distribution of property and debt, and name change. Even if there are issues in dispute, it is a good idea to prepare a proposed final judgment of divorce to take to court. Prepare the judgment as if you have won the case and received all of the relief that you requested in your complaint. For instance, if you are asking for custody of minor children, you would prepare the judgment as if the court had decided to give physical custody of the children to you. If you are asking for a specific amount of child support or alimony, you can put this specific amount in the proposed final judgment of divorce. However, if you have made a general request for those types of relief and are waiting for the judge to decide on the specific amount, you will leave it blank. See **Final Default Judgment of Divorce (Form 21)**.

At the end of the hearing, the judge probably will issue his or her opinion orally. The judge will decide what relief to order and will sign the proposed judgment you brought to the hearing or change it, if that is necessary.

Note: *If the defendant does not attend the hearing, you must send the defendant a copy of the final default judgment of divorce.* Send the judgment by both regular *and* certified mail, return receipt requested, within seven days of the date that it is signed by the judge. Use the **Cover Letter to Defendant—Final Default Judgment of Divorce (Form 21A)**. Always keep the copy received from the court for yourself. You must also file with the court a **Certification of Service (Form 16)**, which proves that you have served a copy of the **Final Default Judgment of Divorce (Form 21)**, signed by the judge, on the defendant.

In *Chapter 6: Issues after Final Judgment* on page 101, we explain some steps that you may need to take to enforce your order. Please read that chapter now to see if any of the suggestions apply to you.

If the defendant seeks to vacate the default after a judgment is signed, the defendant can apply to the court to set aside the default judgment and allow him or her to participate in the case. If the defendant gives a good explanation of why he or she failed to participate in the case, the court may vacate the default judgment of divorce and give the defendant an opportunity to file an **Answer and Counterclaim for Divorce (Form 14A, 14B, 14C,** or **14D)**. If the defendant files a counterclaim with his or her answer, refer to page 69 for an explanation of how to properly prepare and file an **Answer to Counterclaim for Divorce (Form 15A)**.

Checklist for Filing Documents and Table of Documents— Forms 17 through 21A

Review your documents and package for the court to make sure that:

❑ You have filled in the appropriate blanks on the documents that you are sending or hand delivering to the court.

❑ You have left blank the sections of the judgment of divorce that must be filled out by the judge.

❑ Every document is signed and dated, except for those left blank for the judge's signature.

❑ You are sending an original and two copies of all documents to the court.

❑ You have prepared and enclosed a self-addressed, stamped envelope (an envelope with your name, address, and postage on it) for the court to use to return filed copies to you.

❑ You have the right amount of postage on your package. We suggest that you have your package weighed and stamped at the post office. The court will not deliver mail with inadequate postage.

❑ You have kept at least one extra copy of all documents for your records.

❑ After mailing documents to the defendant, you have saved any green return receipt cards with signature or any envelopes stamped by the post office as "unclaimed" or "refused."

❑ You have marked on your calendar:

○ The date two weeks from the date you sent your documents to the court with a note to call the court clerk if you have not received a date for your default hearing.

○ The date from the court for your hearing.

○ The date 20 days before the date of your hearing so that you are reminded to file your notice of application for equitable distribution before that date.

Forms for Chapter 4: Getting a Default Judgment
Forms 17 through 21A

Form #	Title of Form	Instructions
	Documents to Be Filed When Defendant Is in Default	
17	Request to Enter Default Judgment and Supporting Certification and Certification of Service (Form 16)	Send original and two copies to court for filing. At the same time, send one copy of each form to defendant via regular *and* certified mail, return receipt requested.
17A	Filing Letter to Court— Request to Enter Default Judgment	Send to court with Forms 16, 17, and 18. Keep a copy for your records.
18	Certification of Non-Military Service (attach certificates from each branch of the military)	Send to court with Forms 16, 17, and 17A for filing. At the same time, send one copy to defendant via regular *and* certified mail, return receipt requested.
19	Notice of Default Divorce Hearing and Certification of Service (Form 16)	Send to defendant via regular *and* certified mail, return receipt requested. Keep a copy for your records.
19A	Cover Letter to Defendant—Notice of Default Divorce Hearing	Send to defendant via regular *and* certified mail, return receipt requested, with Form 20. Keep a copy for your records.
20	Notice of Application for Equitable Distribution and Certification of Service (Form 16)	**20 days or more before the date of your divorce hearing**, submit an original and one copy to the court for filing, along with Form 16. **Send to defendant via regular *and* certified mail, return receipt requested, in time to ensure that defendant receives the document 20 days or more prior to the hearing.**
20A	Filing Letter to Court— Notice of Application for Equitable Distribution	Send to defendant with Forms 20 and 16. Keep a copy for your records.
21	Final Default Judgment of Divorce	Bring to court on day of default hearing. Judge will probably sign and file it **in court on that day**. Send filed copy to defendant with Form 16 within seven days of the date it is signed by the judge. File form 16 with the court. Keep a copy for your records.
21A	Cover Letter to Defendant—Final Default Judgment of Divorce	Send to defendant with Form 21. Keep a copy for your records.

Chapter 5:
Going to Court When the Defendant Is Not in Default

This chapter will explain the different steps of the court process where the defendant has answered the complaint and you are going to trial, including:

- The case management conference to decide how and when the case will proceed.
- Discovery—exchanging documents and obtaining financial and other information related to the case, and obtaining professional assessments of assets such as pensions, businesses, and real estate.
- The Early Settlement Program to assist the parties in coming to an agreement about how to divide property and decide on child support and alimony before going to trial.
- Mediation for parties who disagree about custody of the children.
- The divorce hearing.
- The final judgment of divorce.

This chapter will cover Forms 22 through 26A.

Chapter 5:
Going to Court When the Defendant Is Not in Default

Defendant Files an Answer

In *Chapter 4: Getting a Default Judgment* on page 75, we described the steps you need to take when the defendant has not filed a written answer and is in default. In this chapter, we describe how a divorce will proceed when the defendant has filed an answer. If you and your spouse can reach a settlement or agreement about contested issues, see the instructions on page 91 and read about uncontested divorces. If you do not agree on the issues, you will proceed through the steps below. We explain the process for both contested and uncontested divorces.

If you have not organized all of the divorce papers that you have prepared so far, please do that now, following the suggestions on page 80. You may not need all of the documents suggested, but organizing will save you time if you are asked to produce a document or prove that you took some action.

Case Management Conference

If the defendant answers the complaint, you are ready to move ahead. The court is supposed to schedule a case management conference within 30 days after the court receives the last pleading. (The last pleading is either the answer to the complaint or, if there is a counterclaim along with the answer, your answer to the defendant's counterclaim.) At the case management conference, the judge and the attorneys for the parties, or the parties themselves if they do not have attorneys, meet in court and discuss the following subjects:

- The contested issues in the case (the issues about which the parties disagree).
- What forms of pre-trial *discovery* the parties may use and time frames for discovery. (Discovery is the process by which each party finds out information about the other party's situation as related to the case. See *Discovery Before Trial* on page 88.)
- A trial date or a date for a second case management conference to set a trial date.
- A date for the early settlement program, if the judge thinks the case is appropriate for that program.
- Other miscellaneous matters related to the case.

At the case management conference, the parties do not testify and the judge does not review evidence. The purpose of the conference is for the parties to introduce the judge to the case, identify the areas of disagreement, and estimate how long each side will take to present his or her case. The conference can be conducted by telephone.

If either party has an attorney, the attorney must participate. The parties do not have to be present unless the court specifically orders them to be present, but they must be available to answer questions by telephone if necessary. If you are representing yourself, you must be present.

At the end of the conference, the judge will sign a case management order that sets a discovery schedule, a date for a second case management conference, a date to appear before an early settlement panel, or a trial date.

Discovery Before Trial

The discovery process permits each party to gather relevant information about the other party. A discovery schedule explains how and when the parties will exchange necessary documents and information concerning the case. For example, during discovery in a divorce case, parties may send each other requests for the production of documents such as tax returns or other financial documents. Discovery also gives the parties the opportunity to obtain professional evaluations of the value of assets such as pensions, businesses, and real estate. In some cases, it may be difficult to get this information without the assistance of an attorney. You should seek the assistance of an attorney if you need to have assets evaluated. If you do not know which documents to ask for, or are unsure what investments your spouse has, it is a good idea to first send *interrogatories* that ask questions about those issues. Interrogatories are written questions that ask for written answers. Interrogatories can also ask for documents. Once you receive the answers to the interrogatories, you may have a better idea of which documents you need to see.

If your spouse refuses to provide you with relevant information, you can ask the court for assistance by filing a motion to compel your spouse to comply with your request for discovery.

There are a number of other ways in which the parties can collect information. However, discovery tools are often difficult to use without the assistance of an attorney. If you feel you will need substantial information about your spouse, or if you are having trouble getting necessary information from your spouse, you should speak with an attorney.

Parents' Education Program

If the parties have minor children, they are required to attend a one-time seminar on parenting, which explains how the court process works and discusses parents' responsibilities for their children and children's needs during and after the divorce. When you filed your complaint, you were required to pay an additional $25 fee for this program. If you do not attend the program, the judge may consider that when making decisions about custody and parenting time/visitation. Parties with restraining orders are exempt from the program, and the judge can excuse you from the program if you demonstrate a good reason for not participating.

Mediation of Custody and Parenting Time/Visitation

When parties cannot agree about custody or parenting time/visitation, the court may send the parties to a court mediator to try to resolve these issues. The court can send parties to a mediator any time after the complaint has been filed. Parties with temporary or permanent domestic violence restraining orders are exempt from the requirement of participating in mediation. The Family Division of the Superior Court offers at least two types of mediation in every county, Matrimonial Early Settlement Panels (MESPs) and Custody/Visitation Mediation. Some counties have additional services available for other family-related disputes. For more information about these services, contact the Complementary Dispute Resolution (CDR) coordinator for your county. See *www.judiciary.state.nj.us/services/cdr.htm*.

Parties who are ordered to participate in mediation are required to attend a mediation orientation program. They may then be required to attend an initial mediation session. These sessions are closed to the public. The mediator may terminate the session at any time if he or she thinks that it is appropriate according to certain guidelines and rules. In addition, the mediator or either party may petition the court to remove the case from mediation at any time if they can show good cause to do this. Unless the parties otherwise consent, no disclosure made by a party during a mediation session may be used as evidence against that party in a hearing or trial.

Matrimonial Early Settlement Programs (MESPs)

After the parties have submitted their pleadings (complaint, answer, counter-claim, and answer to counterclaim) and their case information statements, a judge will review the case and decide whether the parties should try to settle the case. If the judge decides that this might be helpful, he or she will send the parties to a matrimonial early settlement program (MESP). The parties must appear and try to work out their differences. Five days or more prior to the hearing, the parties must submit a written description of the issues that remain unsettled in their case. If either party fails to appear, the court may require the party who failed to appear to pay the counsel fees of the other party, or the court may dismiss that party's pleadings.

The MESP normally consists of volunteer attorneys who review the case, listen to the parties' requests, suggest a solution to the contested issues, and recommend a settlement agreement. If the parties cannot agree on a settlement, they may be referred to post-MESP mediation (see below), or they will have a trial. Parties can settle some issues and still have a trial on the issues that they cannot resolve. The statements made by the parties in the mediation cannot be used against either of them in a later trial. If your spouse attempts to use something that you said in mediation against you when you are in front of the judge at a trial, you should object to this and let the judge know that this is the reason you are objecting.

Post-MESP Mediation and Post-MESP Complementary Dispute Resolution

If the parties are unable to settle their case in MESP, the court may issue an order for additional mediation or another form of post-MESP Complementary Dispute Resolution (CDR). [For a description of the most common types of CDR, see *Explanation of Dispute Resolution Alternatives* (Form 2A).] The court order will state that the parties can select a mediator from a statewide-approved list of mediators or select another individual to conduct this post-MESP CDR. If you and your spouse choose your own mediator, you must do so within seven days of the receipt of the order.

You must then participate in the post-MESP program for at least two hours. You may participate voluntarily for longer, but you are not required to do this. In the first hour, the mediator will prepare the case. In the second hour, you and your spouse will participate in actually mediating the contested issues in your case.

Custody and Parenting Time/Visitation Plan

If you and your spouse disagree about custody and parenting time/visitation issues, you will each have to file a *Custody and Parenting Time/Visitation Plan* **(Form 22)** with the court within 75 days after the defendant answers the complaint. Use the *Filing Letter to Court—Custody and Parenting Time/Visitation Plan* **(Form 22A)**. If the defendant files a counterclaim, the plans must be filed within 75 days after you file your answer. In your plan, you must give the court certain information, including:

- What type of custody you are seeking and why.
- The schedule you propose for parenting time/visitation.
- Whether or not you seek to share decision-making about the child(ren).

Requests for Relief Before the Divorce is Final—*Pendente Lite* Motions

Because the divorce process can take several months or longer, the parties often need help from the court before the final judgment of divorce has been entered. If you need to get a temporary order related to custody of the children or financial support while the case is going on, you must file a motion. A motion for relief before the judge decides your divorce case is called a motion for *pendente lite* relief. This manual does not explain how to obtain this relief. You should talk to a lawyer if you need to file such a motion.

Trial or Settlement

Notice of Trial Date

After you have gone to the case management conference, participated in mediation, completed discovery, and have, in some cases, appeared before a Matrimonial Early Settlement Panel, you should receive a notice from the court about your trial date. If you do not receive a notice within 10 days of completing pre-trial discovery, call the court. You will get this notice even if you have been able to work out a settlement agreement. By the time you get your trial notice, you will have a good idea about what issues you and your spouse can agree upon and what issues you simply cannot work out.

Uncontested Divorce—Getting a Divorce When There Are No Contested Issues

How to Prepare for a Hearing

If you have settled all of the issues by the time you attend your hearing, the judge will hold a brief hearing and ask you a few basic questions. If the divorce is uncontested (meaning that both parties agree about everything or that neither party has filed any objections to the claims made by the other party), the court often will ask you a few questions to establish the truth of the statements in your complaint. The court will probably not ask for testimony or evidence to be presented. You must still appear on the trial date even if you feel there is nothing that needs to be discussed.

Documents to Take to Your Hearing

You will need to file an updated *Family Part Case Information Statement (CIS)* *(Form 3A)* with supporting financial documents if your financial situation has changed substantially since you filed your complaint, if you are the plaintiff, or since you filed your answer and counterclaim, if you are the defendant.

When you go to your hearing, take the following documents with you:

- All papers that have been filed with the court, including:
  - The *Complaint for Divorce* (Form 1A, 1B, 1C, or 1D) *and Attached Certification*.
  - The *Certification of Insurance* (Form 2).
  - The *Certification of Notification of Complementary Dispute Resolution* (Form 2B).
  - The *Answer and Counterclaim for Divorce* (Form 14A, 14B, 14C, or 14D), if there is one.
  - The *Family Part Case Information Statement (CIS)* (Form 3A) for each party, if these documents were required and were filed.
- Your marriage certificate, if you have one.
- Your children's birth certificates and Social Security numbers, if they have them.

- Recent pay stubs, if you work.
- Any settlement agreement.
- Your proposed *Consent Order—Final Judgment of Divorce* (Form 24), explained below.
- Any property deeds that need to be signed. (If the defendant comes to court, the judge can order him or her to sign them.)

The judge should have copies of all of the documents in the court file, except for the proposed final consent judgment of divorce, which you will prepare before you appear in court for your hearing. However, if the judge is missing one of documents listed above and you come prepared with your own forms, you can show the court your copy of the document, which may help the judge grant your divorce more quickly.

Preparing the Proposed *Consent Order—Final Judgment of Divorce*

The court order that legally ends your marriage is called a *final judgment of divorce*. That court order describes the resolution of the issues that you have raised in your divorce complaint, such as custody, child support, alimony, equitable distribution of property and debt, and name change. When both parties agree to be bound by an agreement, the final judgment will be called a *consent judgment* or *consent order*. You will need to prepare a proposed final consent judgment for your hearing. In it, you will write down the agreement you and your spouse have reached on every issue on which you agree. Do not sign the consent judgment before the hearing. You and your spouse and the judge will all sign it after the judge reviews it at the hearing and asks you questions about it. Your answers to those questions must be given in court on the record.

What to Expect at the Hearing

A few days before your hearing, call to confirm the time and date of the hearing and the name of the judge assigned to your case. On the day of the hearing, arrive about 10-15 minutes early so that you will have to time to collect your thoughts before you have to go before the judge. When you arrive at the courthouse, look for a court officer or other staff person and give him or her the title and docket number of your case and your name.

If the defendant is not present for the hearing, the judge will make sure the defendant was served properly with the summons and complaint. If a sheriff's officer served the summons and complaint, the court should already have a copy of the proof of service. If no proof of service has been filed, you may have to show the court proof that the defendant was served, such as a return receipt.

The court may ask you a few questions to determine that everything in the complaint is true to the best of your knowledge. The court normally assumes that you are telling the truth in your pleadings, unless your spouse contests something that you have said. It is important to listen carefully to the judge's questions and answer them truthfully. If you do not understand a question, ask the judge or the attorney or other party to repeat the question.

If you have requested that the court grant a name change, the judge will ask you why you are changing your name. The judge must make sure that you are not changing your name to get out of any debts owed to creditors or to avoid any criminal charges that may have been filed against you. Answer these questions in a clear and straightforward manner. If you do not understand the judge's question, ask the judge to repeat or explain the question to you.

If there is a separate settlement agreement, it will be attached to the actual judgment of divorce. The judge will also want to make certain that both of you have read the settlement agreement and understand all of it before you and the defendant sign the agreement. If you are agreeing to the divorce by way of a consent judgment, the judge will ask each party or each party's attorney to read the agreement carefully before you and the defendant sign it. If you do not understand something in the agreement, or if you disagree with something, you do not have to sign the agreement.

Contested Divorce—Getting a Divorce When There Are Contested Issues

How to Prepare for Trial

The issues that you were *not* able to work out or settle in your divorce case will have to be decided by a judge at a hearing or a trial. If you do not have a lawyer, you may want to consider trying mediation before going to trial if you have not done so. Or you may want to reconsider hiring an attorney if that is possible. See page 4 to learn how to find a mediator or a lawyer.

At the trial, each party can testify or explain his or her view of the situation. Both parties may present evidence that is relevant to the issues in the case, such as documents, pictures, or videotapes, and bring other witnesses to testify. If there are many disputed issues, the trial will be long and could take several days. If there are only a few issues that need to be decided, the trial may only take a few hours.

Often it is not the grounds for divorce that are disputed by the husband or wife, but the other issues, such as who will get custody, how much alimony one spouse will pay to the other, or who gets what part of the property.

Witnesses at the Trial

Prepare for your trial by considering whether or not you need to bring any witnesses to testify on your behalf. For instance, if custody is a disputed issue, you may want to have another person, such as a relative, friend, teacher, or day care provider, come and testify about how you have been the primary caretaker of your child and are more actively involved in your child's life than your spouse, if that is the case.

How to Get Witnesses to Come to Court to Testify—Subpoenas

You do not have to serve a subpoena on a witness who is willing to come to court voluntarily. However, if your witness is not cooperative or reliable, then you should serve that witness with a subpoena, an order from the clerk of the court demanding that the witness attend the trial and give testimony. A subpoena can also order a witness to bring documents to the trial. A witness must receive a subpoena five days or more before the trial date.

You prepare the subpoena, and the law gives you the authority to sign the name of the clerk of the court. See *Subpoena Duces Tecum ad Testificandum* **(Form 23)**. You must also pay the witness a fee for traveling to and from the hearing. As of the time of publication of this manual, this fee is $2 per day for witnesses who live in the same county as that of the court. For witnesses who must travel from another county, the fee is an additional $2 per day for every 30 miles of travel.

Documents to Take to Your Trial

Your list should begin with the same documents listed above for an uncontested hearing. (See page 91.) If your financial situation has changed substantially, you will need to update your *Family Part Case Information Statement (CIS)* **(Form 3A)** and supporting documents.

You may also need other documents or evidence, depending upon what issues are disputed.

- *Example 1:* If you and your spouse are disputing who should have custody, you will need to present witnesses and other evidence, such as documents, to support your claim that it is in your child's best interest to live with you and not your spouse. For example, if your spouse has been convicted of a crime or has a domestic violence restraining order against him or her, this is relevant to whether or not he or she should have custody. You should take to court a copy of the judgment of conviction or the domestic violence restraining order. You can also take witnesses, such as friends, relatives, clergy, health care providers, child care providers, etc., to testify about your parenting skills.
- *Example 2:* If your spouse is refusing to help pay for joint credit card bills, you should take copies of those bills to show that the credit cards were used to buy household items.

Preparing the Final Judgment of Divorce

Even if there are issues in dispute, it is a good idea to prepare a proposed final judgment of divorce to take to court. Prepare the judgment as if you have won the case and received all of the relief that you requested in your complaint. For instance, if you are asking for custody of the minor children, you should prepare the judgment as if the court has decided to give physical custody of the children to you. If you are asking for a specific amount of child support or alimony, you can put this specific amount in the proposed final judgment of divorce. However, if you have made a general request for those types of relief and are waiting for the judge to decide on the specific amount, then you should leave that part blank. See *Final Judgment of Divorce* **(Form 25)**.

If there are many issues that are being presented at trial and if the trial is a long one, the judge may "reserve" his or her decision. This means that, instead of giving a decision at the end of the trial, the judge will call you back to court at a later date and deliver the decision in open court, or send the decision to you after he or she has completed it. This often happens in cases where there are complicated issues concerning division of property or debts.

What to Expect at Your Divorce Trial

At the trial, you and your spouse will present witnesses and evidence that support your requests for relief in the *Complaint for Divorce* **(Form 1A, 1B, 1C,** or **1D)**. The plaintiff presents his or her side of the story first. After each of the plaintiff's witnesses testifies, the defendant or the defendant's attorney, if he or she has one, can *cross-examine* those witnesses. This means asking them questions about what they said. Then the defendant presents his or her case, and the plaintiff or the plaintiff's attorney can cross-examine those witnesses. The judge can also ask questions of any of the witnesses. The most important instruction for a witness in a courtroom is to remember to listen to the question asked and to give only the answer to that question and no more.

Final Judgment of Divorce

The *Final Judgment of Divorce* **(Form 25)** is the court order that ends your marriage and grants your divorce. It will also include any other relief the court orders. The judge can use the order form that you or the defendant submitted and write on it any changes to the proposed order, or the judge can prepare a new order. The judge can also request that plaintiff or defendant or plaintiff's or defendant's attorney prepare a new order, but judges are usually more likely to ask an attorney to prepare a proposed order. After the hearing, the party that prepares the proposed order is required to send a copy of the proposed order to the other party and to the court. The party receiving the proposed order has five days from the time he or she receives it to notify the judge and the other party of any objections to anything that is incorrectly stated in the order, or to add anything that has been left out. If the objecting party does not make those objections known to the court, the judge will sign the order as written. It is a good idea to take notes about what the judge orders while he or she is ordering it in court so that you can remember what the order should say.

If you are asked to prepare the proposed judgment and submit it to the court, use the *Cover Letter to Judge—Five-Day Rule* **(Form 26)**, and send a copy of the letter and the proposed judgment to your spouse at the same time that you send it to the court. Your spouse will have five days to object in writing to anything that he or she disagrees with in the order that you have prepared. The judge will then have you both come back to court, after reviewing his or her notes or listening to the tape of your hearing, and will decide whether the language in the judgment is correct.

If both you and your spouse appear without attorneys and you are awarded most of what you asked for in your complaint, the judge could ask you to write the order. Even if the judge or someone else writes the order, you will want to make sure it is accurate. Compare the order to your notes. If you think the judge has written something in the order that is not the same as what the judge said at the end of the trial, ask the judge about it immediately. Below are things that will be set out in the judgment:

- The amount of alimony and how and when it will be paid.
- How the property and debts are to be divided. (If any property deeds need to be signed, make sure the defendant signs them or ask the judge to order him or her to sign them.)
- The amount of child support and how and when it will be paid.
- Who will have legal and physical custody of the children.
- A change of name, if requested. (If you request a name change in the divorce, make sure that you get an official court seal on your order. You will need this when you request that agencies use your new name. If you are not sure whether or not you have an official seal, ask the judge or the court clerk. If you choose to use the new name, you will need to show your final order to any agencies that you want to use it. Agencies to consider contacting include your bank, the Social Security office, and the Motor Vehicle Commission.)

Checklist for Filing Documents and Table of Documents— Forms 22 through 26A

Review your documents and package for the court to make sure that:

❑ You have filled in the appropriate blanks on the documents that you are sending or hand-delivering to the court.

❑ You have left blank the sections of the documents that must be filled out by the judge.

❑ You have filed an updated *Family Part Case Information Statement (CIS)* **(Form 3A)**, with supporting financial documents, if your financial situation has changed substantially since the time you filed your complaint.

❑ You have sent subpoenas and a fee for travel at least five days before the date of your hearing to all uncooperative witnesses, demanding that those witnesses attend the hearing and testify.

❑ Every document is signed and dated, except for those left blank for the judge's signature.

❑ You are sending an original and two copies of all documents to the court.

❑ You have prepared and enclosed a self-addressed, stamped envelope (an envelope with your name, address, and postage on it) for the court to use to return filed copies to you.

❑ You have the right amount of postage on your package. We suggest that you have your package weighed and stamped at the post office. The court will not accept mail with inadequate postage.

❑ You have kept at least one extra copy of all documents for your records.

❑ After mailing documents to the defendant, you have saved any green return receipt cards with signature or any envelopes stamped by the post office as "unclaimed" or "refused."

❑ You have marked on your calendar:

   o The date 75 days after the date that the defendant answers the complaint or, if the defendant files a counterclaim, the date 75 days after you file your answer to the counterclaim, in order to file your *Custody and Parenting Time/Visitation Plan* **(Form 22)** on time.

   o The date 10 days from the date that you complete your pre-trial discovery, so you can call the court if you have not received a notice from the courts about your trial date by that time.

Forms for Chapter 5: Going to Court When Defendant Is Not in Default
Forms 22 through 26A

Form #	Title of Form	Instructions
22	Custody and Parenting Time/Visitation Plan	**75 days or less after the answer or (if there is one) answer to counter-claim is filed,** submit original and one copy to court for filing. Send a copy to the other parent via regular *and* certified mail, return receipt requested, with Form 16.
22A	Filing Letter to Court—Custody and Parenting Time/Visitation Plan	Send to court with Form 22. Send a copy to other parent with copy of Form 22.
23	Subpoena Duces Tecum ad Testificandum	Send a copy to witness via regular *and* certified mail, return receipt requested, with fee (see page 94). Keep a copy for your records.
23A	Cover Letter to Witness—Subpoena Duces Tecum ad Testificandum	Send to witness via regular *and* certified mail, return receipt requested, with Form 23.
24	Consent Order—Final Judgment of Divorce	Send filed copy to ex-spouse via certified or regular mail, along with Form 16, within seven days of the date that it is signed by the judge. Keep a copy for your records.
25	Final Judgment of Divorce	Send filed copy to ex-spouse via certified or regular mail along with Form 16 within seven days of the date that it is signed by the judge. Keep a copy for your records.
26	Cover Letter to Judge—Five-Day Rule	If court instructs one party to prepare another order, send to the court as soon as possible after hearing and send copy to spouse.
26A	Cover Letter—Final Judgment of Divorce	Send to court with Form 26. Send copy to spouse. Instructs spouse that he or she has five days within which to give the court notice of his or her objections to the form of the order. If there are no objections, the court will sign and file. After signed and sent to preparing party, preparing party should send a copy to ex-spouse within seven days of date order was signed.

Chapter 6:
Issues After Final Judgment

This chapter explains:

- Things that cannot be changed after the judgment has been signed—property sale or property and debt distribution.
- Things that can be changed if circumstances change—custody, alimony, and child support.
- Practical steps you need to take to enforce your court order.
- Documents you need to send to the defendant.

Chapter 6:
Issues After Final Judgment

Some things in the final judgment of divorce can be changed if the parties' situations change. However, some things cannot be changed, except in extraordinary circumstances.

It is unlikely that any decisions regarding the division of property or debts will be changed. However, child support, alimony, custody, and visitation arrangements can always be reexamined if the parties can demonstrate a good reason for a change. For example, if one party becomes unable to work or the other gets a substantial increase in salary, you could ask the court to reconsider the child support order. Or, if the non-custodial parent believes that something has changed to prevent the custodial parent from being able to take care of a child, he or she could request a change in custody. If both parties agree to a change, they can draft a consent order and submit it to the court. If the court accepts the agreement, the judge and both parties will sign the consent order.

If the parties do not agree to a change, the party seeking a change must file an application called a *motion* with the court. If you want to file a motion for relief after the final judgment of divorce, go to the courthouse where your divorce was granted and ask for the forms to file a post-judgment motion. Court personnel may be able to give you forms and information about how to prepare your motion. You can also find these forms on the Judiciary Web site at *www.judiciary.state.nj.us/forms.htm*.

Practical Steps After Your Final Judgment of Divorce

Once the judge signs the final judgment of divorce, you might have to take some steps to make sure you get what the court ordered. Below are some things you may have to do, depending upon your situation. The list below does not cover every situation; rather, it highlights a few of the most common actions that parties might have to take after a divorce.

- You must send the defendant a signed copy of the final judgment of divorce.
- In addition to the copy of the final judgment signed by the judge at your hearing, you might want to get a certified copy of your judgment. This is a document that has a special raised seal on it. It is a good idea to get a certified copy because you may need it in order to change certain documents or to get a marriage license, should you want to remarry.
- If the judge ordered that you can use another name, you might want to notify Social Security, the Motor Vehicle Commission, IRS, and other agencies or institutions. You should call them to see if they require a certified copy of your judgment.

- If the judge ordered the defendant to pay debts on credit cards or to pay premiums on insurance policies, you should make sure that the defendant is doing what he or she was ordered to do. The regular payment of insurance premiums is very important. If the defendant is not paying them, you might have to pay them yourself until you can go back to court to get your money back from the defendant and get the defendant to make future payments. You will have to file a motion to enforce the final judgment. To do this, you must go to the courthouse where your divorce was granted. Most counties have forms for this kind of motion, and the court can also give you information on how to prepare the papers. You can also find these forms on the Judiciary Web site at ***www.judiciary.state.nj.us/prose/10483.pdf***. You may need help from a lawyer to do this. If your divorce judgment divided real estate, you will have to fill out deeds and other documents in order to transfer property according to the divorce judgment. You may also need to fill out titles or other documents for the transfer of automobiles and other kinds of personal property. You may need help from a lawyer to do this.
- Child support is usually administered through the probation department. The judge will generally direct his or her staff to make certain that probation gets a copy of this order. However, you may also want to notify probation and send them a copy of your order to make sure that the child support case is promptly opened and enforced.

If you file a motion to enforce your divorce judgment and the court finds that the defendant is in violation of the order, the court can order a number of punishments. For example, the court can order that your spouse do what he or she has been ordered to do within a certain time period or risk having the court issue a warrant for arrest. You should be aware that it is hard to execute a warrant on a defendant, especially one who doesn't live in New Jersey. It is even harder to enforce a court order on a defendant who lives outside of the United States. However, you can often send a message to your ex-spouse by filing a motion to enforce a court order and exposing the fact that he or she is not complying with the directions of the court. A lawyer can prepare and file a motion for you, but this does not necessarily guarantee that your ex-spouse will abide by the court order in the future. Unfortunately, ex-spouses often repeatedly try to avoid their responsibilities, which results in a loss of time and money in trying to actually get what you were awarded in your divorce.

Conclusion and Reminder

The beginning of this manual contains several warnings about getting a divorce on your own. These same warnings apply to complicated issues that arise after the final judgment of divorce. This manual is not meant as a substitute for legal assistance and representation. If you have any further questions concerning any aspect of your divorce, please consult Appendix C on page 115 and contact the lawyer referral service of your county bar association. If you are a low-income New Jersey resident, you may be eligible for legal help from a Legal Services office in your area. See Appendix D on page 117 for a list of Legal Services programs in New Jersey. You may also be eligible for free legal advice from LSNJ-LAW™, Legal Services of New Jersey's statewide, toll-free legal hotline. The hotline telephone number is 1-888-LSNJ-LAW (1-888-576-5529). Hotline hours are Monday through Friday, 8 a.m. to 5:30 p.m. If you are income-eligible, a Legal Services attorney can give you more information and advice over the telephone. If you are not eligible for Legal Services, the hotline will refer you to other possible resources.

Glossary

AFFIDAVIT—A written or printed statement of facts signed by the party making the statement and witnessed by a person who is authorized by the government to administer oaths and attest to the fact that the signature on a document is authentic.

ALIMONY—Money paid by one spouse to the other spouse after the divorce to help the other spouse continue to live the way he or she lived while married. Also called *spousal support*.

ANSWER—The document filed by the defendant in response to the complaint filed by the plaintiff. The answer admits to the statements in the plaintiff's complaint that are true and denies the statements that are false. An answer can also include a *counterclaim*.

ANSWER TO COUNTERCLAIM—The document filed by the plaintiff in response to the defendant's counterclaim.

APPEARANCE—Where a defendant who is not represented by an attorney does not file an answer to a complaint, he or she may enter a general appearance by signing a document called an acknowledgment of service and returning it to the plaintiff. (See page 46 for an explanation of the procedure for using an acknowledgment of service.) Where a defendant who is represented by an attorney does not file an answer to a complaint, his or her attorney may still make an appearance by sending a letter to the court or filing a motion informing the court that he or she is representing the defendant in the matter before the court.

ARBITRATION—An arbitration proceeding is more formal than a mediation session (see *mediation*). Like mediation, arbitration relies on an impartial third party to decide issues in a case. The parties can decide that the arbitrator's decision will be binding on them, meaning that they cannot question those decisions or appeal them. While an arbitrator may decide some issues within a divorce case, only the judge hearing the divorce case can decide whether or not to grant the divorce.

BEST INTERESTS INVESTIGATION—In family actions where the court determines that the custody of children is a genuine and substantial issue, the court may order an investigation to determine what is in the best interests of the child regarding custody and parenting time/visitation. This investigation is often referred to as a best interests investigation. Depending on what factors are in dispute, a best interests investigation may consist of either a home inspection, a social investigation, or both. The investigation may be done by any member of the staff of the Family Division of the Superior Court. The purpose of the investigation is to provide the court with information that corresponds to the list of factors designated by New Jersey law as being relevant to a determination of the best interests of the child in a custody dispute. (See page 27.)

CAUSE OF ACTION—The grounds or reason for your divorce.

CHANCERY DIVISION—The Division of the Superior Court of New Jersey where lawsuits asking primarily for non-money-related relief are filed and heard by the court. The Chancery Division includes, among other parts, the Family Part, where divorces are filed and heard by the court. See *Family Part*.

CHILD SUPPORT—Financial support provided by the non-custodial parent to the custodial parent to help support the children.

CERTIFICATION—A written or printed statement of facts which supports a request for relief to the court. The party who makes the statement of facts swears at the end of the document that everything stated is true to the best of that party's knowledge. Unlike an affidavit, this document does not require the signature of an authorized witness, such as a notary public.

CIVIL ACTION—A lawsuit that involves non-criminal claims against a party.

COBRA—Consolidated Omnibus Reconciliation Act of 1986. The law that requires employers to offer a continuation or extension of health coverage in certain instances where coverage under that plan would normally end, such as when an employee is terminated from or leaves a job.

COMPLAINT—The document that begins a lawsuit in the civil division of the New Jersey Superior Court. A complaint must set forth claims that give the party being sued a general idea about what he or she is being sued for. The party who files the complaint is known as the *plaintiff*.

CONSENT JUDGMENT—A judgment signed by the plaintiff, the defendant, and the judge, where the plaintiff and defendant reach an agreement with respect to all of the terms included in the consent judgment. When the parties come to an agreement of this type, they usually avoid having to participate in a trial or hearing.

CONSENT ORDER—See *consent judgment*.

CONTESTED DIVORCE—A divorce where the defendant contests or objects to the things that the complaint states happened—for example, that the defendant committed adultery or was cruel to the plaintiff in some way, or where the defendant objects to something the plaintiff is asking for in the complaint, such as custody, support, or property. Contested divorces usually take more time and end up being more complicated.

COUNT—The term that refers to the plaintiff's or defendant's statement of the fact or facts in a complaint or counterclaim, which give him or her a right to relief from the court. For example, a divorce complaint or counterclaim might contain two counts, with one demonstrating facts supporting a right to a divorce based on extreme cruelty and the other demonstrating facts supporting a right to a divorce based on desertion.

COUNTERCLAIM—A complaint filed by the defendant against the plaintiff as a part of the defendant's response to the plaintiff's complaint. In a divorce action, the defendant will often file a counterclaim with his or her *answer*.

CROSS-EXAMINATION—The process by which the attorney for the opposing party (or the opposing party if he or she does not have an attorney) asks questions of the party and the party's witnesses about the answers that they have given to questions asked during *direct examination*. For example, after each of the plaintiff's witnesses testifies, the defendant (or the defendant's attorney, if he or she has one) can cross-examine those witnesses. The plaintiff or the plaintiff's attorney can also cross-examine the defendant's witnesses. The questions asked on cross-examination must refer to something that the witness has said in response to questions on direct examination. The judge can also ask questions of any of the witnesses during cross-examination.

CROSS-MOTION—A type of document that can be filed in response to a motion. Another type of response to a motion is a certification in opposition to that motion. Unlike a certification in opposition to a motion, a cross-motion usually concerns a subject different from that of the motion originally filed by the opposing party.

CUSTODIAL PARENT—This term usually refers to the parent with whom the child physically resides. In situations where the child resides most of the time with this parent but also resides part of the time with the other parent, the custodial parent may be referred to as the parent of primary residence.

CUSTODY—This term refers to the right of a natural or adoptive parent to the care, control, and maintenance of his or her natural or adopted child. Custody is awarded to a parent or parents in a divorce or custody proceeding. See also *physical custody, legal custody,* and *sole custody.*

DEFAULT JUDGMENT—In the context of a divorce case, when the defendant is properly served with a complaint and fails to respond to it by filing an answer in the time allowed, the plaintiff can request that the court grant him or her judgment by default in his or her favor against the defendant.

DEFENDANT—The party who is sued by a plaintiff in a civil lawsuit is called the defendant. The accused in a criminal lawsuit is also referred to as the defendant.

DIRECT EXAMINATION—The process by which a party or a party's witness answers questions asked by either a judge (if the party has no attorney) or by his or her attorney (if the party is represented by an attorney). After direct examination is completed, the opposing party or the attorney for the opposing party is permitted to ask questions of the party's witnesses on *cross-examination* (see above). The person asking the questions is not supposed to "lead the witness" (to use words in the question that give the answer to the question). The judge also can ask questions of any of the witnesses during direct examination.

DISCOVERY—The disclosure of facts, documents, and other information by the defendant and plaintiff to each other before the hearing or trial takes place.

DISMISS—To discontinue or end a lawsuit without any further consideration or hearing.

DISSOLUTION—Another term for the act of terminating a marriage by way of divorce.

DIVORCE—The legal end of a marriage by way of a judgment or order of a court.

DOCKET NUMBER—The number assigned by the clerk of the court to a case when it is filed with the court, so that it may be easily identified and located. Always include your docket number on all letters and documents sent to the court or to the other parties in the case.

EQUITABLE DISTRIBUTION—Under New Jersey law, this term refers to the concept of equitably (fairly) dividing marital property (the property of a husband and wife acquired by either of them during their marriage) or marital debt (debt incurred by either the husband or wife during the marriage) as a part of a divorce case.

EVIDENCE—Testimony, written documents, material objects, or other things presented at a trial for the purpose of proving the existence or nonexistence of a fact.

EXHIBIT(S)—This term refers to papers, documents, or other objects that are either attached to an affidavit or a certification in order to support factual statements made in the affidavit or certification. The term also refers to papers, documents, or other objects presented to the court during a trial or hearing in order to support facts that are presented by testimony or other evidence at that trial or hearing.

FAMILY PART—The part of the Chancery Division of the Superior Court where lawsuits involving subjects that arise out of family-type situations are filed and heard by the court.

FAULT-BASED DIVORCE—A divorce based on a specific reason (ground or fault). See page 20 for a list of the grounds for a fault-based divorce.

FINAL JUDGMENT OF DIVORCE—The court order that legally ends your marriage. That court order describes the resolution of the issues that you have raised in your divorce complaint, such as custody, child support, alimony, equitable distribution of property and debt, and name change.

FINAL RESTRAINING ORDER—A court order issued after the filing of a domestic violence complaint and a hearing where both the plaintiff and defendant have had an opportunity to appear and present evidence, or where the defendant waives the right to a hearing and admits to having committed an act of domestic violence. This type of court order normally restrains the defendant from having any type of contact with the plaintiff. Under New Jersey law, final restraining orders remain in force indefinitely or until either plaintiff or defendant apply to the court and convince the court, by way of evidence, to dissolve the order.

HEARING—A public proceeding in a court in which witnesses are heard, evidence is presented, and the parties to the lawsuit are present and have a right to be heard. There is no jury present. This proceeding is formal, but somewhat less formal than a *trial*.

INTERROGATORIES—Written questions sent to the opposing party as a part of the discovery process prior to the trial or hearing.

JUDGMENT—The court order that represents the court's written decision in a lawsuit. The judgment should be signed and dated on the date that the case is decided.

LEGAL CUSTODY—The parent with legal custody of a child is responsible for making important decisions concerning the child, such as where the child should go to school and what kind of medical care the child should get. It is common for both parents to retain legal custody of the child, even where only one parent has physical custody.

LEGAL RELIEF—What you are asking the court to order in your complaint or your motion.

LITIGANTS—The name given to persons named in and participating in a lawsuit. See also *parties*.

MEDIATION—The act of attempting to resolve a dispute or disputes with the help of a neutral third party before a trial or hearing.

MOTION—An application to the court for some sort of *legal relief*. Motions are usually filed after an order has been entered in a lawsuit, although sometimes they can be filed at the beginning of a lawsuit in place of an answer to a complaint or with an answer to a complaint. Sometimes a motion requests new relief, which changes the original order or judgment. Sometimes a motion is a request to enforce something in an existing order, which one party is ordered to do but is failing to do. The party who files the motion papers with the court is referred to as the *moving party*. The moving party files his or her papers and the other party (the *responding party*) is permitted to respond to the request for relief by either agreeing to it or opposing it. The responding party may also file a *cross-motion* asking for his or her own independent relief from the court. The moving party is permitted to respond to the cross-motion by opposing it or consenting to it. The court usually hears (considers) motions and cross-motions at the same time, and decides either to grant or deny them. If the court decides to grant the motion and/or cross-motion, the court will issue a new order that enforces or changes the prior order. If the court denies the motion and/or cross-motion, the court issues an order stating that the motion and/or cross-motion is/are denied and clarifying that the original order remains in effect. If the court grants one of the applications and denies the other, it will issue a new order to that effect.

MOVING PARTY—The party who files *motion* papers with the court.

NO-FAULT DIVORCE—A divorce based on the fact that you and your spouse have experienced irreconcilable differences for a period of six months or more, or based on the fact that you and your spouse have been living separate and apart in different places for 18 consecutive months or more.

NON-CUSTODIAL PARENT—This term refers to the parent who does not have the child physically living with him or her. In situations where the child resides most of the time with the other parent but also resides part of the time with this parent, the non-custodial parent may be referred to as the parent of secondary residence.

NOTARY PUBLIC—A public officer whose function it is to administer oaths and to certify by his or her official seal that the signature of the party taking the oath is authentic. Law offices, banks, and real estate offices often have employees who may also be notaries public.

ORDER—The court's written decision in a lawsuit, signed and dated on the date that the case is decided. See also *judgment*.

PARTIES—The plaintiff(s) and defendant(s) named in a civil lawsuit.

PENDENTE LITE—Latin term meaning pending or during the actual progress of the lawsuit or litigation. In the context of a divorce, "*pendent lite* relief" is relief that one or more of the parties applies for before the final judgment of divorce is entered.

PERSONAL PROPERTY—Possessions such as cars, appliances, TV sets, sound equipment, jewelry, expensive tools, furniture, etc.

PHYSICAL CUSTODY—The parent with physical custody is the parent the child lives with most of the time. This parent is also called the *custodial parent* or the parent of primary residence.

PLAINTIFF—The party who begins a civil lawsuit by filing a complaint.

PROOF OF SERVICE—A document filed with the court that proves the date on which documents were formally served on a party in a court action.

PRO SE—Acting as one's own lawyer. In Latin, "for oneself."

PUBLIC BENEFITS—Financial assistance that some low-income families or individuals may be eligible to receive from the local, county, or federal government. Public benefits include the different forms of welfare such as Temporary Aid to Needy Families (TANF), General Assistance (GA), and Emergency Assistance (EA). Other benefits include food stamps, Medicaid, and Supplemental Security Income (SSI).

QDRO—Qualified Domestic Relations Order. A QDRO is a special type of order prepared by an expert and approved by the court that is used to divide a private or state pension. Division of a federal pension requires the use of a different type of order, called a Court Order Approved for Processing (COAP).

REAL PROPERTY—Land and any building on the land, such as a house. Real property is also called real estate.

RESPONDING PARTY—The party who responds to the *moving party*'s request for relief by agreeing to it, opposing it, or filing a cross-motion to respond to it.

SERVICE/SERVICE OF PROCESS—The legal term for delivering to or leaving with a person who is a party to a lawsuit, a summons or writ, or other official court paper which gives that party notice of the fact that someone has filed a lawsuit against him or her. The purpose of service is to give the party reasonable notice of when and where the proceedings concerning the lawsuit will take place, so that he or she will have the opportunity to appear at that proceeding and be heard. In the context of a divorce, the initial service of process refers to delivering to or leaving with the defendant a copy of the divorce complaint and a summons. The most common type of service is personal service, which means simply delivering to or leaving with an actual person. Other types of service are called *substituted service*, which refers to giving the party notice by way of mailing the papers, leaving the papers with someone else, or publishing a notice of the lawsuit in a newspaper.

SHERIFF—In New Jersey, an office of the court that employs officers who perform official duties such as providing security to the courthouse and serving process on litigants. See *service/service of process.*

SOLE CUSTODY—The term that describes the legal result when a court awards both legal and physical custody to only one of the parents of a child. Sole custody is usually ordered only in situations where one parent is missing or absent or has been found legally unfit to parent a child. The parent with no custodial rights may still be awarded visitation or parenting time with the child, but it is likely to be limited and supervised.

SPOUSAL SUPPORT—Technically, this term refers to support paid by a husband or wife to his or her spouse while they are separated but before they are divorced. However, sometimes this term is used in place of the term alimony although, technically, alimony refers to support paid after the divorce. See also *alimony.*

SUBSTITUTED SERVICE—See *service.*

SUBPOENA—A command issued from the clerk of the Superior Court to appear at a certain time and place to give testimony in a hearing or trial.

SUBPOENA DUCES TECUM—A command issued from the clerk of the Superior Court to appear at a certain time and place to give testimony in a hearing or trial and to produce at the hearing or trial specific papers and documents related to the case.

SUMMONS—The official notice to the defendant that someone has filed a lawsuit against him or her. It also tells the defendant where and how he or she must respond to the complaint and how long he or she has to respond.

TEMPORARY RESTRAINING ORDER—A court order issued against the defendant after the plaintiff alone gives testimony to a municipal or Superior court judge concerning alleged abuse by the defendant. A temporary restraining order makes a preliminary finding before there is a full hearing, based only on the plaintiff's testimony, that the plaintiff is in need of this protection. The order requires the defendant to stay away from the plaintiff and not communicate with him or her in any way. It also orders both parties to appear at a final restraining order hearing within 10 days or less of the date of the order and give testimony to the court.

TESTIMONY—The statement of a witness in court under oath.

TEVIS CLAIM—A claim by one spouse for damages for a personal injury caused by the other spouse. This type of claim is named for the case that brought this concept to the attention of the court.

TRIAL—A public proceeding in which witnesses may testify, evidence may be presented, and the parties to the lawsuit have a right to testify. In addition, a jury may be present at a trial. In the context of a divorce case, it is extremely rare to have a jury decide anything except issues involving personal injury of one spouse by the other. A trial is usually more formal than a *hearing*.

UNCONTESTED DIVORCE—A divorce where the defendant spouse does not object to the things the plaintiff says happened in the marriage or does not object to anything the plaintiff is asking for in the complaint.

WORKERS COMPENSATION—A fixed award given to an employee who is injured in the course of employment, or whose injuries arise out of the employment. In return for getting a fixed amount of money from his or her employer, the employee gives up his or her right to sue the employer for damages for pain and suffering and compensation due to the employer's alleged negligence.

Appendix A:
Where to File Your Divorce

Atlantic County
Superior Court, Chancery Division, Family Part
Atlantic County Civil Courthouse
Direct Filing
1201 Bacharach Blvd.
West Wing
Atlantic City, NJ 08401
(609) 345-6700

Bergen County
Superior Court, Chancery Division, Family Part
Justice Center, 119
10 Main Street
Hackensack, NJ 07601
(201) 527-2300

Burlington County
Superior Court, Chancery Division, Family Part
Burlington County Central Processing Office
Attention: Dissolution Intake
Courts Facility, 1st floor
49 Rancocas Rd.
Mount Holly, NJ 08060
(609) 518-2621

Camden County
Superior Court, Chancery Division, Family Part
Camden County Family Division
Hall of Justice, 2nd floor
101 S. 5th Street
Camden, NJ 08103-4001
(856) 379-2204

Cape May County
Walk-Ins:
Superior Court, Chancery Division, Family Part
9 N. Main Street
Cape May Court House, NJ 08210
(609) 463-6600
Mailing Address:
Superior Court, Chancery Division, Family Part
4 Moore Road
Cape May Court House, NJ 08201
(609) 463-6600

Cumberland County
Superior Court, Chancery Division, Family Part
Dissolution Direct Filing Unit
Cumberland County Courthouse
Broad and Fayette Streets
Without Fee:
P.O. Box 866
With Fee:
P.O. Box 816
Bridgeton, NJ 08302
(856) 451-8000

Essex County
Superior Court, Chancery Division, Family Part
Family Finance Unit
Wilentz Justice Complex
1st floor, Room 111
212 Washington Street
Newark, NJ 07102
(973) 693-6710

Gloucester County
Superior Court, Chancery Division, Family Part
Finance Unit
Family Court Facility
P.O. Box 881
Woodbury, NJ 08096
(856) 686-7464

Hudson County
Superior Court, Chancery Division, Family Part
Hudson Fee Office, Family
101 Administration Building,
595 Newark Avenue,
Jersey City, NJ 07306
(201) 795-6636

Hunterdon County
Superior Court, Chancery Division, Family Part
Family Case Management Office
Hunterdon Justice Center
65 Park Avenue
Flemington, NJ 08822
(908) 237-5919

Mercer County

Superior Court, Chancery Division, Family Part
Family Case Management Office
175 S. Broad Street, 2nd Floor
P.O. Box 8068
Trenton, NJ 08650-0068
(609) 571-4400

Middlesex County

Superior Court, Chancery Division, Family Part
Family Part Intake Reception Team
Family Courthouse
120 New Street
P.O. Box 2691
New Brunswick, NJ 08903-2691
(732) 981-3014

Monmouth County

Filing with Fee:
Superior Court, Chancery Division, Family Part
Courthouse
71 Monument Park
P.O. Box 1260
Freehold, NJ 07728
(732) 677-4050
Filing without Fee:
Superior Court, Chancery Division, Family Part
Courthouse
71 Monument Park
P.O. Box 1252
Freehold, NJ 07728
(732) 677-4050

Morris County

Superior Court, Chancery Division, Family Part
Morris County Family Division/Matrimonial
Courthouse
P.O. Box 910
Morristown, NJ 07963-0910
(973) 656-4362

Ocean County

Superior Court, Chancery Division, Family Part
Ocean County Central Intake
Justice Complex, Room 210
120 Hooper Avenue
P.O. Box 2191
Toms River, NJ 08753
(732) 929-2037

Passaic County

Passaic County Superior Court,
Chancery Division, Family Part
Matrimonial Unit
County Administration Building, 8th floor
401 Grand Street
Paterson, NJ 07505
(973) 247-8535 or 8477

Salem County

Superior Court, Chancery Division, Family Part
Salem County
Family Court Intake
92 Market Street
P.O. Box 223
Salem, NJ 08079
(856) 935-7510, Ext. 8264

Somerset County

Superior Court, Chancery Division, Family Part
Family Case Management Office
Courthouse, 2nd floor
P.O. Box 3000
Somerville, NJ 08876-1262
(908) 231-7600

Sussex County

Superior Court, Chancery Division, Family Part
Sussex County Family Division
Sussex County Judicial Center
43-47 High Street
Newton, NJ 07860
(973) 579-0630

Union County

Superior Court, Chancery Division, Family Part
Dissolution Assignment Office
New Annex Building, 1st Floor
Elizabethtown Plaza
Elizabeth, NJ 07207
(908) 659-3311

Warren County

Superior Court, Chancery Division, Family Part
Family Division Dissolution Unit
Courthouse
413 Second Street
P.O. Box 900
Belvidere, NJ 07823-1500
(908) 475-6163

Appendix B:
Sheriff's Offices

Atlantic County
Sheriff's Office
Criminal Courthouse Complex
4997 Unami Blvd.
Mays Landing, NJ 08330
(609) 909-7221

Bergen County
Sheriff's Office
Justice Center
10 Main Street
Hackensack, NJ 07601-3672
(201) 646-2200

Burlington County
Sheriff's Office Building
2nd Floor
49 Rancocas Road
P.O. Box 6000
Mount Holly, NJ 08060
(609) 265-5127

Camden County
Sheriff's Office
Courthouse, Room 100
520 Market Street
Camden, NJ 08102-0769
(856) 225-5470

Cape May County
Sheriff's Office
4 Moore Road, DN 301
Cape May Courthouse, NJ
08210-1601
(609) 463-6426

Cumberland County
Sheriff's Office
220 N. Laurel Street.
P.O. Box 677
Bridgeton, NJ 08302
(856) 451-4449, Ext 108

Essex County
Sheriff's Office
Veterans' Building
50 West Market Street
Newark, NJ 07102
(973) 621-4081

Gloucester County
Sheriff's Office
Criminal Justice Complex
Attention: Civil Process
70 Hunter Street
P.O. Box 376
Woodbury, NJ 08906-7376
(856) 384-4600

Hudson County
Sheriff's Office
G15 Administrative Building
595 Newark Avenue
Jersey City, NJ 07306
(201) 795-6336 (process service)

Hunterdon County
Sheriff's Office
8 Court Street
P.O. Box 2900
Flemington, NJ 08822-2900
(908) 788-1166

Mercer County
Sheriff's Office
Civil Courthouse
175 S. Broad Street
P.O. Box 8068
Trenton, NJ 08650-0068
(609) 989-6100 (option #2)

Middlesex County
Sheriff's Building
701 Livingston Avenue
P.O. Box 1188
New Brunswick, NJ 08903
(732) 745-3366

Monmouth County
Sheriff's Office
Veteran's Memorial Building
50 East Main Street
Freehold, NJ 07728-1263
(732) 431-7138

Morris County
Sheriff's Office
Court and Washington Streets
P.O. Box 900
Morristown, NJ 07963-0900
(973) 285-6600

Ocean County
Sheriff's Office
Justice Complex
120 Hooper Avenue
P.O. Box 2191
Toms River, NJ 08754
(732) 929-2044 (civil process)

Passaic County
Sheriff's Office
Courthouse
Attention: Civil Process
77 Hamilton Street
Paterson, NJ 07505
(973) 881-4200

Salem County
Sheriff's Office
94 Market Street
Salem, NJ 08079
(856) 935-7510, Ext. 8606

Somerset County
Sheriff's Department
20 Grove Street
P.O. Box 3000
Somerville, NJ 08876-1262
(908) 231-7140 (option #2)

Sussex County
Sheriff's Office
39 High Street
Newton, NJ 07860-1741
(973) 579-0850

Union County
Sheriff's Office
County Administration Building
1st Floor
10 Elizabethtown Plaza
Elizabeth NJ 07202-6001
(908) 527-4450

Warren County
Sheriff's Office
413 2nd Street
Belvidere, NJ 07823
(908) 475-6393

Appendix C:
Lawyer Referral Services

Atlantic County Bar Association
NJ Lawyer Referral Service
Atlantic County Court House
1201 Bacharach Blvd.
Atlantic City, NJ 08401
(609) 345-3444; Fax: (609) 345-6279
atcobara@aol.com

Bergen County Bar Association
NJ Lawyer Referral Service
15 Bergen Street
Hackensack, NJ 07601
(201) 488-0044; Fax: (201) 488-0073

Burlington County Bar Association
NJ Lawyer Referral Service
45 Grant Street
Mount Holly, NJ 08060
(609) 261-4862; Fax: (609) 261-5423
www.burlcobar.org

Camden County Bar Association
NJ Lawyer Referral Service
800 Cooper Street, Suite 103
Camden, NJ 08102
(856) 482-0618; Fax: (856) 482-0637
www.camdencountybar.org

Cape May County
NJ Lawyer Referral Service
Rt. 9, Main Street, P.O. Box 425
Cape May Court House, NJ 08210
(609) 961-0172; Fax: (609) 778-1193
CapeMayCtyBarAsn@aol.com

Cumberland County
NJ Lawyer Referral Service
P.O. Box 2031
Vineland, NJ 08362-2031
(856) 825-2001; Fax: (856) 692-2317

Essex County Bar Association
NJ Lawyer Referral Service
354 Eisenhower Parkway
Plaza 2
Livingston, NJ 07039
(973) 533-6775; Fax: (973) 533-6720

Gloucester County Bar Association
NJ Lawyer Referral Service
Justice Complex, P.O. Box 338
Woodbury, NJ 08096
(856) 848-4589; Fax: (856) 384-9580

Hudson County Bar Association
NJ Lawyer Referral Service
583 Newark Ave.
Jersey City, NJ 07306
(201) 798-2727; Fax: (201) 798-1740

Hunterdon County
NJ Lawyer Referral Service
P.O. Box 573
Annandale, NJ 08801
(908) 735-2611; Fax: (908) 735-0305
Director: Suzanne Vrancken
suzannevrancken@yahoo.com

Mercer County Bar Association
NJ Lawyer Referral Service
1245 Whitehorse-Mercerville Road
Suite 420
Hamilton, NJ 08619-3894
(609) 585-6200; Fax: (609) 585-5537
Francine@mercerbar.com
www.mercerbar.com

Middlesex County Bar Association
NJ Lawyer Referral Service
87 Bayard Street
New Brunswick, NJ 08901
(732) 828-0053
jcowles@mcbalaw.com

Monmouth Bar Association
NJ Lawyer Referral Service
Court House
Freehold, NJ 07728
(732) 431-5544; Fax: (732) 431-2843
tmaciewicz.monmouthbar@horizon.net

Morris/Sussex County Bar Association
NJ Lawyer Referral Service
28 Schuyler Place
Morristown, NJ 07960
(973) 267-5882; Fax: (973) 605-8325

Ocean County Bar Association
NJ Lawyer Referral Service
Courthouse
P.O. Box 381
Toms River, NJ 08753
(732) 240-3666; Fax: (732) 240-4907

Passaic County Bar Association
NJ Lawyer Referral Service
Courthouse
Hamilton Street
Paterson, NJ 07505
(973) 278-9223

Salem County Bar Association
NJ Lawyer Referral Service
(856) 935-5629

Somerset County Bar Association
NJ Lawyer Referral Service
Courthouse
20 N. Bridge Street
P.O. Box 1095
Somerville, NJ 08876
(908) 685-2323; Fax: (908) 685-9839
hwendover@somersetbar.com

Union County Bar Association
NJ Lawyer Referral Service
Courthouse, 1st Floor
Elizabeth, NJ 07207
(908) 353-4715; Fax: (908) 354-8222

Warren County Bar Association
NJ Lawyer Referral Service
413 Second Street
Belvidere, NJ 07823
(908) 387-1835

Appendix D:
New Jersey Legal Services Offices

State Coordinating Program
Legal Services of New Jersey
P.O. Box 1357
Edison, NJ 08818-1357
(732) 572-9100
www.LSNJ.org
LSNJ-LAW™ toll-free, statewide legal hotline:
1-888-LSNJ-LAW (1-888-576-5529)
www.LSNJLAW.org

Regional Legal Services Programs

Central Jersey Legal Services

Mercer County	(609) 695-6249
Middlesex County—New Brunswick	(732) 249-7600
Middlesex County—Perth Amboy	(732) 324-1613
Union County	(908) 354-4340

Essex-Newark Legal Services (973) 624-4500

Legal Services of Northwest Jersey

Hunterdon County	(908) 782-7979
Morris County	(973) 285-6911
Somerset County	(908) 231-0840
Sussex County	(973) 383-7400
Warren County	(908) 475-2010

Northeast New Jersey Legal Services

Bergen County	(201) 487-2166
Hudson County	(201) 792-6363
Passaic County	(973) 523-2900

Ocean-Monmouth Legal Services

Monmouth County—Freehold	(732) 866-0020
Monmouth County—Long Branch	(732) 222-3338
Ocean County	(732) 341-2727

South Jersey Legal Services

Atlantic County	(609) 348-4200
Burlington County	(609) 261-1088
Camden County—Camden	(856) 964-2010
Cape May County	(609) 465-3001
Centralized Intake	1-800-496-4570
Consumer Law Unit	(856) 429-8291
Cumberland/Salem Counties	(856) 451-0003
Gloucester County	(856) 848-5360

Appendix E:
New Jersey Judiciary Ombudsman
Telephone Directory

Atlantic/Cape May
Kathleen Obringer . . . . . . (609) 345-6700, ext.3346 . . Fax: (609) 343-2142

Bergen
Mary Demmer . . . . (201) 527-2263 . . . . Fax: (201) 371-1111

Burlington
Nancy Gramaglia . . . . . . (609) 518-2530 . . . . Fax: (609) 518-2539

Camden
Nalo Brown . . . . (856) 379-2238 . . . . Fax: (856) 379-2278

Cumberland/Gloucester/Salem
Sandra Lopez-Palmer . . . . (856) 453-4538 . . . . Fax: (856) 455-9490

Essex
Shazeeda Samsudeen . . . . (973) 693-5728 . . . . Fax: (973) 693-5726

Hudson
Janice Kidney . . . . (201) 217-5399 . . . . Fax: (201) 795-6603

Mercer
Judith Irizarry . . . . (609) 571-4205 . . . . Fax: (609) 571-4208

Middlesex
Sylvia O'Connor . . . . . . (732) 981-3371 . . . . Fax: (732) 565-2955

Monmouth
Theresa Romano . . . . . . (732) 677-4209 . . . . Fax: (732) 677-4363

Morris/Sussex
Kim Daniels Walsh . . . . . (973) 656-3969 . . . . Fax: (973) 656-3942

Ocean
Ann Marie Fleury . . . . . . (732) 929-2042 . . . . Fax: (732) 288-7606

Passaic
Renita McKinney . . . . . . (973) 247-8651 . . . . Fax: (973) 247-8012

Somerset/Hunterdon/Warren
Aime Alonzo-Serrano . . . . (908) 203-6135 . . . . Fax: (908) 231-7632

Union
Leslie Santora . . . . (908) 282-4841 . . . . Fax: (908) 659-3880

Forms

The following section contains all of the forms referenced in this manual. Please refer to the Forms Table of Contents on page 121.

Forms Table of Contents

Form #	Title of Form	Page
8B	Filing Letter to Court—Acknowledgment of Service	171
9	Letter of Inquiry to Defendant's Friends, Family, or Employers	172
9A	Letter of Inquiry to MVC	173
9B	Letter of Inquiry to Postmaster	174
9C	Letter of Inquiry to Military	175
9D	Letter of Inquiry to Military (Army)	176
9E	Letter of Inquiry to Military (Air Force)	177
9F	Letter of Inquiry to Military (Navy)	178
9G	Letter of Inquiry to Military (Marine Corps)	179
9H	Letter of Inquiry to Military (Coast Guard)	180
10A	Request for Order Permitting Substituted Service on a Special Agent and Supporting Certification	181
10B	Order Permitting Substituted Service on a Special Agent	184
10C	Filing Letter to Court—Request for Substituted Service	187
11A	Request for Order Permitting Service by Publication and Supporting Certification	188
11B	Order Permitting Service by Publication	191
11C	Filing Letter to Court—Request for Service by Publication	194
12	Notice of Order of Publication	195
12A	Cover Letter to Newspaper Requesting Publication	196
12B	Filing Letter to Court Re: Certification of Publication	197

Form #	Title of Form	Page
13	Consent Order Extending Time to Answer	198
13A	Filing Letter to Court—Consent Order Extending Time to Answer	200
14A	Answer and Counterclaim for Divorce Based on Separation and Attached Certification	201
14B	Answer and Counterclaim for Divorce Based on Desertion and Attached Certification	206
14C	Answer and Counterclaim for Divorce Based on Extreme Cruelty and Attached Certification	211
14D	Answer and Counterclaim for Divorce Based on Irreconcilable Differences and Attached Certification	217
14E	Filing Letter to Court—Answer and Counterclaim for Divorce	222
15A	Answer to Counterclaim for Divorce	223
15B	Filing Letter to Court—Answer to Counterclaim for Divorce	225
16	Certification of Service	226
17	Request to Enter Default Judgment and Supporting Certification	228
17A	Filing Letter to Court—Request to Enter Default Judgment	230
18	Certification of Non-Military Service	232
19	Notice of Default Divorce Hearing	235
19A	Cover Letter to Defendant—Notice of Default Divorce Hearing	236
20	Notice of Application for Equitable Distribution	237
20A	Filing Letter to Court—Notice of Application for Equitable Distribution	240

Name _____
(Plaintiff's name, address, and telephone number)

Address _____

_____

Telephone _____

Plaintiff, *Pro Se*

SUPERIOR COURT OF NEW JERSEY
CHANCERY DIVISION—FAMILY PART

_____ COUNTY
(County where divorce complaint is filed)

DOCKET NO. FM _____
(Assigned by the court at the time of the filing of the complaint)

Name: _____
              Plaintiff

vs.

Name: _____
              Defendant

CIVIL ACTION

**COMPLAINT FOR
DIVORCE
Based on Separation**

1. Plaintiff, _____,
                    (Your name)

resides at _____
                (Your address)

_____,

City of _____, County of _____,

and State of _____.

2. Plaintiff was lawfully married to _____,
                        (Your spouse's name)

the defendant herein, on _____
                       (Date of your marriage)

in a _____ ceremony performed by
    (Type of ceremony)

_____.
(Name of the person who performed the ceremony)

3.   The parties separated on or about _____.

(Date you began to live apart from your spouse)

Ever since that time and for more than 18 consecutive months, the parties have lived

separately and apart and in different locations. The separation has continued to the

present time and there is no reasonable prospect of reconciliation.

4.   At the point at which plaintiff and defendant had lived separately for 18

months, plaintiff was a *bona fide* resident of the State of New Jersey. Since that date, and

for more than one year before the date of filing this complaint, plaintiff has continued to

be a *bona fide* resident of this state.

5.   At the point at which plaintiff and defendant had lived separately for at least

18 months, plaintiff lived at _____

(Your address at the point at which you had been separated from your spouse for 18 months)

_____,

City of _____, County of _____,

and State of _____.

6.   The defendant, _____,

(Defendant's name)

resides at _____

(Defendant's address)

_____.

7.   (Check the appropriate statement below and fill in information where applicable)

_____ A.   No children were born of this marriage.

_____ B.   The following children were born of this marriage:

_____	_____
(Full name)	(Birth date)
_____	_____
(Full name)	(Birth date)
_____	_____
(Full name)	(Birth date)
_____	_____
(Full name)	(Birth date)

8. The plaintiff and defendant in the matter within have been parties to the

following prior actions:

(List any other court cases where you or your spouse are plaintiffs or defendants, such as cases for bankruptcy, personal injury, child support, custody, domestic violence, etc.)

A. _____ _____
   (Caption or title of the case)   (Docket number)

B. _____ _____
   (Caption or title of the case)   (Docket number)

C. _____ _____
   (Caption or title of the case)   (Docket number)

D. _____ _____
   (Caption or title of the case)   (Docket number)

WHEREFORE, plaintiff demands judgment:

(Check the appropriate statement below and fill in information where applicable)

_____ A. Dissolving the marriage between the parties;

_____ B. Ordering that all debts and assets be equitably distributed between the

parties;

_____ C. Ordering that defendant pay child support to plaintiff;

_____ D. Ordering that plaintiff have physical custody of/be the parent of

primary custody for the minor children of the marriage;

_____ E. Ordering that defendant pay alimony to plaintiff;

_____ F. Permitting plaintiff to assume the use of the name of

_____;
(The name that you would like to assume after your divorce)

_____ G. Granting such further relief as the Court may deem just and equitable.

_____
(Plaintiff's signature)   Plaintiff, *Pro Se*

_____
(Plaintiff's name printed)

Dated _____
       (Date on which plaintiff signs this document)

127

CERTIFICATION OF VERIFICATION AND NON-COLLUSION PURSUANT TO R. 4:5-1

1. I am the plaintiff in the foregoing complaint.

2. The allegations of the complaint are true to the best of my knowledge, information, and belief. The complaint is made in truth and good faith and without collusion for the causes set forth therein.

3. The matter in controversy in the within action is not the subject of any other action pending in any court or of a pending arbitration proceeding, nor is any such court action or arbitration proceeding presently contemplated. There are no other persons who should be joined in this action at this time.

I certify that the foregoing statements made by me are true. I am aware that if any of the foregoing statements made by me are willfully false, I am subject to punishment.

_____
(Plaintiff's signature)   Plaintiff, *Pro Se*

_____
(Plaintiff's name printed)

Dated _____
   (Date on which plaintiff signs this document)

Name _____
(Plaintiff's name, address, and telephone number)

Address _____

_____

Telephone _____

Plaintiff, *Pro Se*

SUPERIOR COURT OF NEW JERSEY
CHANCERY DIVISION—FAMILY PART

_____ COUNTY
(County where divorce complaint is filed)

DOCKET NO. FM _____
(Assigned by the court at the time of the filing of the complaint)

Name: _____
Plaintiff

vs.

Name: _____
Defendant

CIVIL ACTION

COMPLAINT FOR DIVORCE
Based on Desertion

1. Plaintiff, _____,
(Your name)

resides at _____
(Your address)

_____,

City of _____, County of _____,

and State of _____.

2. Plaintiff was lawfully married to _____,
(Your spouse's name)

the defendant herein, on _____
(Date of your marriage)

in a _____ ceremony performed by
(Type of ceremony)

_____.
(Name of the person who performed the ceremony)

129

3.   The defendant deserted the plaintiff on or about _____,
(Date on which you were deserted)

ever since which time and for more than 12 consecutive months, defendant has willfully

and continuously deserted plaintiff.

4.   At the point at which defendant deserted plaintiff, plaintiff was a *bona fide*

resident of the State of New Jersey. Since that date, and for more than one year before the

date of filing this complaint, plaintiff has continued to be a *bona fide* resident of this

state.

5.   At the point at which the defendant had deserted plaintiff for at least 12

months, plaintiff lived at _____
(Your address at the time your spouse had deserted you for 12 months)

_____,

City of _____, County of _____,

and State of _____.

6.   The defendant, _____,
(Defendant's name)

resides at _____
(Defendant's address)

_____.

7.   (Check the appropriate statement below and fill in information where applicable)

____ A. No children were born of this marriage.

____ B. The following children were born of this marriage:

_____	_____
(Full name)	(Birth date)
_____	_____
(Full name)	(Birth date)
_____	_____
(Full name)	(Birth date)
_____	_____
(Full name)	(Birth date)

8. The plaintiff and defendant in the matter within have been parties to the following prior actions:

(List any other court cases where you or your spouse are plaintiffs or defendants, such as cases for bankruptcy, personal injury, child support, custody, domestic violence, etc.)

A. _____   _____
        (Caption or title of the case)   (Docket number)

B. _____   _____
        (Caption or title of the case)   (Docket number)

C. _____   _____
        (Caption or title of the case)   (Docket number)

D. _____   _____
        (Caption or title of the case)   (Docket number)

WHEREFORE, plaintiff demands judgment:

(Check the appropriate statement below and fill in information where applicable)

_____ A. Dissolving the marriage between the parties;

_____ B. Ordering that all debts and assets be equitably distributed between the parties;

_____ C. Ordering that defendant pay child support to plaintiff;

_____ D. Ordering that plaintiff have physical custody of/be the parent of primary custody for the minor children of the marriage;

_____ E. Ordering that defendant pay alimony to plaintiff;

_____ F. Permitting plaintiff to assume the use of the name of

_____;
        (The name that you would like to assume after your divorce)

_____ G. Granting such further relief as the Court may deem just and equitable.

_____
(Plaintiff's signature)   Plaintiff, *Pro Se*

_____
(Plaintiff's name printed)

Dated _____
      (Date on which plaintiff signs this document)

CERTIFICATION OF VERIFICATION AND NON-COLLUSION PURSUANT TO R. 4:5-1

1. I am the plaintiff in the foregoing complaint.

2. The allegations of the complaint are true to the best of my knowledge, information, and belief. The complaint is made in truth and good faith and without collusion for the causes set forth therein.

3. The matter in controversy in the within action is not the subject of any other action pending in any court or of a pending arbitration proceeding, nor is any such court action or arbitration proceeding presently contemplated. There are no other persons who should be joined in this action at this time.

I certify that the foregoing statements made by me are true. I am aware that if any of the foregoing statements made by me are willfully false, I am subject to punishment.

_____
(Plaintiff's signature)   Plaintiff, *Pro Se*

_____
(Plaintiff's name printed)

Dated _____
(Date on which plaintiff signs this document)

Name _____

<small>(Plaintiff's name, address, and telephone number)</small>

Address _____

_____

Telephone _____

Plaintiff, *Pro Se*

SUPERIOR COURT OF NEW JERSEY
CHANCERY DIVISION—FAMILY PART

_____ COUNTY

<small>(County where divorce complaint is filed)</small>

DOCKET NO. FM _____

<small>(Assigned by the court at the time of the filing of the complaint)</small>

Name: _____ <center>Plaintiff</center> <center>vs.</center> Name: _____ <center>Defendant</center>	CIVIL ACTION **COMPLAINT FOR DIVORCE** **Based on Extreme Cruelty**

1. Plaintiff, _____,

<small>(Your name)</small>

resides at _____

<small>(Your address)</small>

_____,

City of _____, County of _____,

and State of _____.

2. Plaintiff was lawfully married to _____,

<small>(Your spouse's name)</small>

the defendant herein, on _____

<small>(Date of your marriage)</small>

in a _____ ceremony performed by

<small>(Type of ceremony)</small>

_____.

<small>(Name of the person who performed the ceremony)</small>

3.   The defendant has been guilty of extreme cruelty toward the plaintiff

beginning on or about _____,
(Date when your spouse began his/her acts of cruelty towards you)

continuing from that day until _____.
(Present date or date on which acts of cruelty stopped)

The specific acts of cruelty committed by the defendant are as follows:

A.   On or about _____,
(Date the act of cruelty was committed)

defendant _____
(Describe the act of cruelty)

_____

_____.

B.   On or about _____,
(Date the act of cruelty was committed)

defendant _____
(Describe the act of cruelty)

_____

_____.

C.   On or about _____,
(Date the act of cruelty was committed)

defendant _____
(Describe the act of cruelty)

_____

_____.

D.   On or about _____,
(Date the act of cruelty was committed)

defendant _____
(Describe the act of cruelty)

_____

_____.

4.   It has been more than three months since the last act of extreme cruelty listed above.

5.   At the point at which defendant committed the above-noted acts of cruelty

towards plaintiff, plaintiff was a *bona fide* resident of the State of New Jersey. Since that

date, and for more than one year before the date of filing this complaint, plaintiff has

continued to be a *bona fide* resident of this state.

6. Three months after defendant committed the most recent act(s) of extreme

cruelty towards plaintiff, plaintiff lived at _____
(Your address three months after the most recent act(s) of cruelty)

_____,

City of _____, County of _____,

and State of _____.

7. The defendant, _____,
(Defendant's name)

resides at _____
(Defendant's address)

_____.

8. (Check the appropriate statement below and fill in information where applicable)

____ A. No children were born of this marriage.

____ B. The following children were born of this marriage:

_____	_____
(Full name)	(Birth date)
_____	_____
(Full name)	(Birth date)
_____	_____
(Full name)	(Birth date)
_____	_____
(Full name)	(Birth date)

9. The plaintiff and defendant in the matter within have been parties to the

following prior actions:

(List any other court cases where you or your spouse are plaintiffs or defendants, such as cases for bankruptcy, personal injury, child support, custody, domestic violence, etc.)

A. _____ _____
   (Caption or title of the case)   (Docket number)

B. _____ _____
   (Caption or title of the case)   (Docket number)

C. _____ _____
   (Caption or title of the case)   (Docket number)

D. _____ _____
   (Caption or title of the case)   (Docket number)

WHEREFORE, plaintiff demands judgment:

(Check the appropriate statement below and fill in information where applicable)

_____ A. Dissolving the marriage between the parties;

_____ B. Ordering that all debts and assets be equitably distributed between the

  parties;

_____ C. Ordering that defendant pay child support to plaintiff;

_____ D. Ordering that plaintiff have physical custody of/be the parent of

  primary custody for the minor children of the marriage;

_____ E. Ordering that defendant pay alimony to plaintiff;

_____ F. Permitting plaintiff to assume the use of the name of

_____;
(The name that you would like to assume after your divorce)

_____ G. Granting such further relief as the Court may deem just and equitable.

_____
(Plaintiff's signature)   Plaintiff, *Pro Se*

_____
(Plaintiff's name printed)

Dated _____
(Date on which plaintiff signs this document)

CERTIFICATION OF VERIFICATION AND NON-COLLUSION PURSUANT TO

R. 4:5-1

1. I am the plaintiff in the foregoing complaint.

2. The allegations of the complaint are true to the best of my knowledge, information, and belief. The complaint is made in truth and good faith and without collusion for the causes set forth therein.

3. The matter in controversy in the within action is not the subject of any other action pending in any court or of a pending arbitration proceeding, nor is any such court action or arbitration proceeding presently contemplated. There are no other persons who should be joined in this action at this time.

I certify that the foregoing statements made by me are true. I am aware that if any of the foregoing statements made by me are willfully false, I am subject to punishment.

_____

(Plaintiff's signature)   Plaintiff, *Pro Se*

_____

(Plaintiff's name printed)

Dated _____

(Date on which plaintiff signs this document)

Name _____
(Plaintiff's name, address, and telephone number)

Address _____

_____

Telephone _____

Plaintiff, *Pro Se*

SUPERIOR COURT OF NEW JERSEY
CHANCERY DIVISION—FAMILY PART

_____ COUNTY
(County where divorce complaint is filed)

DOCKET NO. FM _____
(Assigned by the court at the time of the filing of the complaint)

Name: _____
                    Plaintiff

vs.

Name: _____
                    Defendant

CIVIL ACTION

**COMPLAINT FOR
DIVORCE
Based on Irreconcilable
Differences**

1. Plaintiff, _____,
                                (Your name)

resides at _____
                                (Your address)

_____,

City of _____, County of _____,

and State of _____.

2. Plaintiff was lawfully married to _____,
                                                          (Your spouse's name)

the defendant herein, on _____
                                              (Date of your marriage)

in a _____ ceremony performed by
          (Type of ceremony)

_____.
(Name of the person who performed the ceremony)

3. Plaintiff and defendant have experienced irreconcilable differences for a period of six months or more.

4. These irreconcilable differences have caused the breakdown of the marriage.

5. There is no hope of reconciliation between plaintiff and defendant.

6. It appears to the plaintiff that the marriage should be dissolved.

7. For more than one year before the date of filing this complaint, plaintiff has been a *bona fide* resident of this state.

8. At the point at which plaintiff and defendant had experienced irreconcilable differences for a period of six months, plaintiff lived at

_____
(Plaintiff's address at that time)

City of _____, County of _____,

and State of _____.

9. The defendant, _____,
(Defendant's name)

resides at _____
(Defendant's address)

_____.

10. (Check the appropriate statement below and fill in information where applicable)

_____ A. No children were born of this marriage.

_____ B. The following children were born of this marriage:

_____   _____
(Full name)   (Birth date)

_____   _____
(Full name)   (Birth date)

_____   _____
(Full name)   (Birth date)

_____   _____
(Full name)   (Birth date)

11.   The plaintiff and defendant in this matter have been parties to the following prior actions:

(List any other court cases where you or your spouse are plaintiffs or defendants, such as cases for bankruptcy, personal injury, child support, custody, domestic violence, etc.)

A. _____   _____
   (Caption or title of the case)   (Docket number)

B. _____   _____
   (Caption or title of the case)   (Docket number)

C. _____   _____
   (Caption or title of the case)   (Docket number)

D. _____   _____
   (Caption or title of the case)   (Docket number)

WHEREFORE, plaintiff demands judgment:

(Check the appropriate statement below and fill in information where applicable)

_____ A. Dissolving the marriage between the parties;

_____ B. Ordering that all debts and assets be equitably distributed between the parties;

_____ C. Ordering that defendant pay child support to plaintiff;

_____ D. Ordering that plaintiff have physical custody of/be the parent of primary

          custody for the minor children of the marriage;

_____ E. Ordering that defendant pay alimony to plaintiff;

_____ F. Permitting plaintiff to assume the use of the name of

_____;
   (The name that you would like to assume after your divorce)

_____ G. Granting such further relief as the Court may deem just and equitable.

_____
(Plaintiff's signature)   Plaintiff, *Pro Se*

_____
(Plaintiff's name printed)

Dated _____
      (Date on which plaintiff signs this document)

CERTIFICATION OF VERIFICATION AND NON-COLLUSION PURSUANT TO R. 4:5-1

1. I am the plaintiff in the foregoing complaint.

2. The allegations of the complaint are true to the best of my knowledge, information, and belief. The complaint is made in truth and good faith and without collusion for the causes set forth therein.

3. The matter in controversy in the within action is not the subject of any other action pending in any court or of a pending arbitration proceeding, nor is any such court action or arbitration proceeding presently contemplated. There are no other persons who should be joined in this action at this time.

I certify that the foregoing statements made by me are true. I am aware that if any of the foregoing statements made by me are willfully false, I am subject to punishment.

_____
(Plaintiff's signature)   Plaintiff, *Pro Se*

_____
(Plaintiff's name printed)

Dated _____
(Date on which plaintiff signs this document)

Name _____
(Plaintiff's or defendant's name, address, and telephone number)

Address _____

_____

Telephone _____

_____, *Pro Se*
(Plaintiff or defendant)

SUPERIOR COURT OF NEW JERSEY
CHANCERY DIVISION—FAMILY PART

_____ COUNTY
(County where divorce complaint is filed)

DOCKET NO. FM _____
(Docket number of the divorce complaint)

Name: _____
Plaintiff

vs.

Name: _____
Defendant

CIVIL ACTION

**CERTIFICATION
OF INSURANCE
PURSUANT TO
R. 5:4-2(f)**

I, _____, of full age, hereby certify:
(Your name)

1. I am the _____ in the foregoing action for divorce.
(Plaintiff or defendant)

2. The insurance policies listed in this certification represent all of the insurance coverage obtained by or for myself.

3. To the best of my knowledge and belief, none of the insurance coverage listed in this certification was canceled or modified within the ninety days preceding the date of this certification.

(Fill out all applicable sections. If not applicable, write in "not applicable.")

LIFE INSURANCE

Company Name _____   Address _____

_____   _____

Policy No. _____   Beneficiary _____

Face Amount $ _____   _____

Policy Owner _____   Name of Insured _____

_____   _____

                                    Policy Term _____

HEALTH INSURANCE

Insured's Name_____   Address _____

_____   _____

Company Name _____   Group Number _____

_____

I.D. Number _____

Coverage type: Single ☐   Parent/Child Family ☐   Optical ☐
                   Hospital ☐   Major Medical ☐   Dental ☐
                   Diagnostic ☐   Prescription ☐

Check if made available through Employment ☐ or Personally obtained ☐

AUTOMOBILE INSURANCE

Name of Company _____

Company Address _____

Policy Number _____

Policy Expiration Date _____   Vehicle Make _____

Vehicle Model_____   Vehicle Year _____

Coverage Limits _____

Lawsuit Threshold   Yes ☐   No ☐

Umbrella Coverage   Yes ☐   No ☐

Drivers of the Vehicle _____

_____

_____

Lien Holder/Lessor (if applicable) _____

Address of Lien Holder/Lessor _____

_____

Use of the Vehicle   Personal ☐   Business ☐   Personal and Business ☐

HOMEOWNERS INSURANCE

Company Name _____

Company Address _____

_____

Policy No. _____ Policy Expiration: _____

Address of Covered Residence _____

_____

Coverage Limits _____

Umbrella Coverage   Yes ☐   No ☐   Umbrella Coverage $ _____

Mortgage (If applicable)   _____

Address of Mortgagee_____

_____

Rider(s) to Policy   Jewelry ☐   Furs ☐   Artwork ☐   Other ☐

I certify that the foregoing statements made by me are true. I am aware that if any of the foregoing statements made by me are willfully false, I am subject to punishment.

_____
(Plaintiff's or defendant's signature)   Plaintiff or Defendant, *Pro Se*

_____
(Plaintiff's or defendant's name printed)

Dated _____
(Date on which document is signed)

DIVORCE—DISPUTE RESOLUTION ALTERNATIVES TO CONVENTIONAL LITIGATION[*]

Resolving issues concerning your divorce can be costly and difficult. While only a judge can actually grant a divorce, division of your property and your debts, alimony, child support, custody, and parenting time are some of the other issues that may need to be resolved. A judge can decide all issues at trial. However, there are other ways to resolve many of the issues in your divorce. These alternate dispute resolution methods offer greater privacy than resolving the issues in a public trial. They also may be faster and less expensive, and may reduce the level of conflict between you and your spouse during your divorce. You are encouraged to discuss alternative dispute resolution with your lawyer to decide whether these alternate methods may help you and your spouse resolve as many of the issues relating to your divorce as possible before the matter is presented to the judge.

What follows are short descriptions of various forms of alternative dispute resolution that may be used in divorce cases.

MEDIATION[**]

Mediation is a means of resolving differences with the help of a trained, impartial third party. The parties, with or without lawyers, are brought together by the mediator in a neutral setting. A mediator does not represent either side and does not offer legal advice. Parties are encouraged to retain an attorney to advise them of their rights during the mediation process. The mediator helps the parties identify the issues, gather the information they need to make informed decisions, and communicate so that they can find a solution agreeable to both. Mediation is designed to facilitate settlements in an informal, non-adversarial manner. The court maintains a roster of approved mediators or you can use private mediation services. The judge would still make the final determination as to whether to grant the divorce.

ARBITRATION

In an arbitration proceeding, an impartial third party decides issues in a case. The parties select the arbitrator and agree on which issues the arbitrator will decide. The parties also agree in advance whether the arbitrator's decisions will be binding on them or instead treated merely as a recommendation. While an arbitrator may decide issues within a divorce case, the judge would still make the final determination as to whether to grant the divorce.

USE OF PROFESSIONALS

Parties in a divorce may also seek the assistance of other skilled professionals to help resolve issues in a case, such as attorneys, accountants or other financial professionals, and various

---

[*] This constitutes the "descriptive material" referenced in Rule 5:4-2(h) that each divorce litigant must receive and certify as having received.

[**] Note: The adoption of Rule 5:4-2(h) and the promulgation of this descriptive material is in no way intended to indicate any change in the Court's policy, grounded in statutes and court rules, against mediation in any matter in which a temporary or final restraining order has been entered pursuant to the Prevention of Domestic Violence Act.

types of mental health professionals (e.g., psychiatrists, psychologists, social workers, therapists). These professionals may help the parties resolve all of the issues or just specific portions of the case. As with mediation and arbitration, parties making use of these professionals to resolve issues in the divorce are encouraged to consult their attorney for advice throughout this process. While this approach may resolve some issues in the case, the judge would still need to make the final decision to grant the divorce.

COMBINATIONS OF ALTERNATIVES

Depending on your circumstances, it may be helpful for you to use a combination of mediation, arbitration, and skilled professionals to resolve issues in your divorce.

CONCLUSION

Just as every marriage is unique, every divorce is unique as well. The specific circumstances of your divorce determine what method or methods of dispute resolution are best suited to resolve issues in your divorce. You are encouraged to ask your attorney about these alternative dispute resolution methods to resolve issues relating to your divorce.

Using these alternative dispute resolution methods allows you to participate in the decision on those issues, rather than leaving all of the issues to the judge to decide. And presenting the judge with a case in which the only decision remaining is whether to grant the divorce will permit that decision to be made more expeditiously. While the judge must be the one to decide whether to grant the divorce, your role in deciding some or all of the other issues can be enhanced through these alternative dispute resolution methods.

Name _____
(Plaintiff's or defendant's name, address, and telephone number)

Address _____

Telephone _____

_____, *Pro Se*
(Plaintiff or defendant)

SUPERIOR COURT OF NEW JERSEY
CHANCERY DIVISION—FAMILY PART
_____ COUNTY
(County where divorce complaint is filed)

DOCKET NO. FM _____
(Docket number of divorce complaint)

Name: _____ Plaintiff vs. Name: _____ Defendant	CIVIL ACTION **CERTIFICATION OF NOTIFICATION OF COMPLEMENTARY DISPUTE RESOLUTION PURSUANT TO RULE 5:4-2(h)**

1. _____, being of full age, hereby certifies as follows:
   (Plaintiff's or defendant's name)

2. I make this Certification pursuant to New Jersey Court Rule 5:4-2(h).

3. I have read the document entitled "Divorce—Dispute Resolution Alternatives to Conventional Litigation."

4. I thus have been informed as to the availability of dispute resolution alternatives to conventional litigation.

I certify that the foregoing statements made by me are true. I am aware that if any of the foregoing statements made by me are willfully false, I am subject to punishment.

_____
(Plaintiff's or defendant's signature) Plaintiff or Defendant, *Pro Se*

_____
(Plaintiff's or defendant's name printed)

Dated: _____
(Date on which this document is signed)

FAMILY PART CASE INFORMATION STATEMENT

Attorney(s):
Office Address
Tel. No./Fax No.
Attorney(s) for:

vs.	Plaintiff,
	Defendant.

SUPERIOR COURT OF NEW JERSEY
CHANCERY DIVISION, FAMILY PART
COUNTY

DOCKET NO.
CASE INFORMATION STATEMENT
OF _____

NOTICE: This statement must be fully completed, filed and served, with all required attachments, in accordance with Court Rule 5:5-2 based upon the information available. In those cases where the Case Information Statement is required, it shall be filed within 20 days after the filing of the Answer or Appearance. Failure to file a Case Information Statement may result in the dismissal of a party's pleadings.

PART A - CASE INFORMATION:

Date of Statement_____
Date of Divorce (post-Judgment matters)_____
Date(s) of Prior Statement(s)_____
_____
Your Birthdate_____
Birthdate of Other Party_____
Date of Marriage_____
Date of Separation_____
Date of Complaint_____
Does an agreement exist between parties relative to any issue?   [   ] Yes   [   ] No.   If Yes, <u>ATTACH</u> a copy (if written) or a summary (if oral).

ISSUES IN DISPUTE:

Cause of Action_____
Custody_____
Parenting Time_____
Alimony_____
Child Support_____
Equitable Distribution_____
Counsel Fees_____
Other issues [be specific]_____
_____

1. Name and Addresses of Parties:

Your Name   _____
Street Address _____ City_____ State/Zip_____
Other Party's Name _____
Street Address _____ City_____ State/Zip_____

2. Name, Address, Birthdate and Person with whom children reside:
a. Child(ren) From This Relationship

Child's Full Name	Address	Birthdate	Person's Name
_____	_____	_____	_____
_____	_____	_____	_____
_____	_____	_____	_____
_____	_____	_____	_____

b. Child(ren) From Other Relationships

Child's Full Name	Address	Birthdate	Person's Name
_____	_____	_____	_____
_____	_____	_____	_____
_____	_____	_____	_____
_____	_____	_____	_____

148

PART B - MISCELLANEOUS INFORMATION:

1. Information about Employment (Provide Name & Address of Business, if Self-employed)

Name of Employer/Business _____ Address _____

_____

Name of Employer/Business _____ Address _____

_____

2. Do you have Insurance obtained through Employment/Business? [ ] Yes [ ] No. Type of Insurance:
Medical [ ]Yes [ ]No; Dental [ ]Yes [ ]No; Prescription Drug [ ]Yes [ ]No; Life [ ]Yes [ ]No; Disability [ ]Yes [ ]No
Other (explain) _____
Is Insurance available through Employment/Business? [ ] Yes [ ] No Explain:_____

_____

3. ATTACH Affidavit of Insurance Coverage as required by Court Rule 5:4-2 (f) (See Part G)

4. Additional Identification:
Confidential Litigant Information Sheet: Filed [ ]Yes [ ] No

5. ATTACH a list of all prior/pending family actions involving support, custody or Domestic Violence, with the Docket
   Number, County, State and the disposition reached. Attach copies of all existing Orders in effect.

PART C. - INCOME INFORMATION: Complete this section for self and (if known) for spouse.

1. LAST YEAR'S INCOME

	Yours	Joint	Spouse or Former Spouse
1. Gross earned income last calendar (year)	$_____	$_____	$_____
2. Unearned income (same year)	$_____	$_____	$_____
3. Total Income Taxes paid on income (Fed., State, F.I.C.A., and S.U.I.). If Joint Return, use middle column.	$_____	$_____	$_____
4. Net income (1 + 2-3)	$_____	$_____	$_____

ATTACH to this form a corporate benefits statement as well as a statement of all fringe benefits of employment. (See Part G)

ATTACH a full and complete copy of last year's Federal and State Income Tax Returns. ATTACH W-2 statements, 1099's,
Schedule C's, etc., to show total income plus a copy of the most recently filed Tax Returns. (See Part G)
Check if attached: Federal Tax Return [ ]   State Tax Return [ ]   W-2 [ ] Other [ ]

2. PRESENT EARNED INCOME AND EXPENSES

	Yours	Other Party (if known)
1. Average gross weekly income (based on last 3 pay periods – ATTACH pay stubs) Commissions and bonuses, etc., are: [ ] included [ ] not included* [ ] not paid to you.	$_____	$_____

*ATTACH details of basis thereof, including, but not limited to, percentage overrides, timing of payments, etc.
ATTACH copies of last three statements of such bonuses, commissions, etc.

	Yours	Other Party
2. Deductions per week (check all types of withholdings): [ ] Federal [ ] State [ ] F.I.C.A. [ ] S.U.I. [ ] Other	$_____	$_____
3. Net average weekly income (1 - 2)	$_____	$_____

3. YOUR CURRENT YEAR-TO-DATE EARNED INCOME
Provide Dates: From _____ To _____
Number of Weeks_____

1. GROSS EARNED INCOME: $
2. TAX DEDUCTIONS: (Number of Dependents:)

a. Federal Income Taxes   a. $_____

b. N.J. Income Taxes   b. $_____

c. Other State Income Taxes   c. $_____

d. FICA   d. $_____

e. Medicare   e. $_____

f. S.U.I. / S.D.I.   f. $_____

g. Estimated tax payments in excess of withholding   g. $_____

h.   h. $_____

i.   i. $_____

                       TOTAL $_____

3. GROSS INCOME NET OF TAXES $ $_____

4. OTHER DEDUCTIONS   If mandatory, check box

a. Hospitalization/Medical Insurance   a. $_____ [ ]

b. Life Insurance   b. $_____ [ ]

c. Union Dues   c. $_____ [ ]

d. 401(k) Plans   d. $_____ [ ]

e. Pension/Retirement Plans   e. $_____ [ ]

f. Other Plans—specify   f. $_____ [ ]

g. Charity   g. $_____ [ ]

h. Wage Execution   h. $_____ [ ]

i. Medical Reimbursement (flex fund)   i. $_____ [ ]

j. Other: j. $_____ [ ]

                       TOTAL $_____

5. NET YEAR-TO-DATE EARNED INCOME: $_____

NET AVERAGE EARNED INCOME PER MONTH: $_____

NET AVERAGE EARNED INCOME PER WEEK $_____

4. YOUR YEAR-TO-DATE GROSS UNEARNED INCOME FROM ALL SOURCES (including, but not limited to, income from unemployment, disability and/or social security payments, interest, dividends, rental income and any other miscellaneous unearned income)

Source	How often paid	Year to date amount
_____	_____	$_____
_____	_____	$_____
_____	_____	$_____
_____	_____	$_____
_____	_____	$_____
_____	_____	$_____
_____	_____	$_____
_____	_____	$_____
_____	_____	$_____

TOTAL GROSS UNEARNED INCOME YEAR TO DATE $_____

5. ADDITIONAL INFORMATION:

1. How often are you paid? _____

2. What is your annual salary? $ _____

3. Have you received any raises in the current year? [ ]Yes [ ]No. If yes, provide the date and the gross/net amount.
    _____

4. Do you receive bonuses, commissions, or other compensation, including distributions, taxable or non-taxable, in addition to your regular salary? [ ]Yes [ ]No. If yes, explain:_____
    _____

5. Did you receive a bonuses, commissions, or other compensation, including distributions, taxable or non-taxable, in addition to your regular salary during the current or immediate past calendar year? [ ] Yes [ ] No If yes, explain and state the date(s) of receipt and set forth the gross and net amounts received: _____
    _____

6. Do you receive cash or distributions not otherwise listed? [ ] Yes [ ] No If yes, explain. _____
    _____

7. Have you received income from overtime work during either the current or immediate past calendar year? [ ]Yes [ ]No If yes, explain. _____

8. Have you been awarded or granted stock options, restricted stock or any other non-cash compensation or entitlement during the current or immediate past calendar year? [ ]Yes [ ]No If yes, explain. _____
    _____

9. Have you received any other supplemental compensation during either the current or immediate past calendar year? [ ]Yes [ ]No. If yes, state the date(s) of receipt and set forth the gross and net amounts received. Also describe the nature of any supplemental compensation received._____
    _____

10. Have you received income from unemployment, disability and/or social security during either the current or immediate past calendar year? [ ]Yes [ ]No. If yes, state the date(s) of receipt and set forth the gross and net amounts received._____

11. List the names of the dependents you claim:_____

12. Are you paying or receiving any alimony? [ ]Yes [ ]No. If yes, how much and to whom paid or from whom received?   _____

13. Are you paying or receiving any child support? [ ]Yes [ ]No. If yes, list names of the children, the amount paid or received for each child and to whom paid or from whom received. _____
    _____

14. Is there a wage execution in connection with support? [ ]Yes [ ]No If yes explain._____
    _____

15. Has a dependent child of yours received income from social security, SSI or other government program during either the current or immediate past calendar year? [ ]Yes [ ]No. If yes, explain the basis and state the date(s) of receipt and set forth the gross and net amounts received _____
    _____

16. Explanation of Income or Other Information:
    _____
    _____
    _____
    _____
    _____
    _____
    _____

<u>PART D - MONTHLY EXPENSES</u> (computed at 4.3 wks/mo.)

Joint Marital Life Style should reflect standard of living established during marriage. Current expenses should reflect the current life style. Do not repeat those income deductions listed in Part C – 3.

	Joint Marital Life Style Family, including _____ children	Current Life Style Yours and _____ children
SCHEDULE A: SHELTER		
<u>If Tenant:</u>		
Rent……………………………………………………	$_____	$_____
Heat (if not furnished)………………………………….	$_____	$_____
Electric & Gas (if not furnished)…………………………	$_____	$_____
Renter's Insurance…………………………………….....	$_____	$_____
Parking (at Apartment)……………………………………	$_____	$_____
Other charges (Itemize)…………………………………...	$_____	$_____
<u>If Homeowner:</u>		
Mortgage ……………………………………………	$_____	$_____
Real Estate Taxes (if not included w/mortgage payment)…	$_____	$_____
Homeowners Ins (if not included w/mortgage payment)…	$_____	$_____
Other Mortgages or Home Equity Loans ……………………	$_____	$_____
Heat (unless Electric or Gas)…………………………………	$_____	$_____
Electric & Gas………………………………………....	$_____	$_____
Water & Sewer………………………………………	$_____	$_____
Garbage Removal………………………………………	$_____	$_____
Snow Removal…………………………………………	$_____	$_____
Lawn Care………………………………………………	$_____	$_____
Maintenance……………………………………………	$_____	$_____
Repairs…………………………………………………	$_____	$_____
Other Charges (Itemize)………………………………….....	$_____	$_____
<u>Tenant or Homeowner:</u>		
Telephone…………………………………………….....	$_____	$_____
Mobile/Cellular Telephone…………………………………...	$_____	$_____
Service Contracts on Equipment……………………………	$_____	$_____
Cable TV…………………………………………………	$_____	$_____
Plumber/Electrician……………………………………	$_____	$_____
Equipment & Furnishings……………………………………	$_____	$_____
Internet Charges………………………………………....	$_____	$_____
Other (itemize)………………………………………	$_____	$_____
TOTAL	$_____	$_____

SCHEDULE B: TRANSPORTATION		
Auto Payment………………………………………	$_____	$_____
Auto Insurance (number of vehicles:)…………………….....	$_____	$_____
Registration, License…………………………………………	$_____	$_____
Maintenance……………………………………………	$_____	$_____
Fuel and Oil……………………………………………	$_____	$_____
Commuting Expenses………………………………………	$_____	$_____
Other Charges (Itemize)……………………………………	$_____	$_____
TOTAL	$_____	$_____

SCHEDULE C: PERSONAL..

	Joint Marital Life Style Family, including _____children	Current Life Style Yours and _____ children
Food at Home & household supplies...........................	$_____	$_____
Prescription Drugs...	$_____	$_____
Non-prescription drugs, cosmetics, toiletries & sundries......	$_____	$_____
School Lunch..	$_____	$_____
Restaurants..	$_____	$_____
Clothing...	$_____	$_____
Dry Cleaning, Commercial Laundry...........................	$_____	$_____
Hair Care..	$_____	$_____
Domestic Help..	$_____	$_____
Medical (exclusive of psychiatric)*...........................	$_____	$_____
Eye Care*...	$_____	$_____
Psychiatric/psychological/counseling*........................	$_____	$_____
Dental (exclusive of Orthodontic)*...........................	$_____	$_____
Orthodontic*..	$_____	$_____
Medical Insurance (hospital, etc.)*...........................	$_____	$_____
Club Dues and Memberships..................................	$_____	$_____
Sports and Hobbies..	$_____	$_____
Camps...	$_____	$_____
Vacations...	$_____	$_____
Children's Private School Costs..............................	$_____	$_____
Parent's Educational Costs....................................	$_____	$_____
Children's Lessons (dancing, music, sports, etc.).............	$_____	$_____
Baby-sitting..	$_____	$_____
Day-Care Expenses..	$_____	$_____
Entertainment..	$_____	$_____
Alcohol and Tobacco..	$_____	$_____
Newspapers and Periodicals...................................	$_____	$_____
Gifts...	$_____	$_____
Contributions...	$_____	$_____
Payments to Non-Child Dependents..........................	$_____	$_____
Prior Existing Support Obligations this family/other families (specify)...	$_____	$_____
Tax Reserve (not listed elsewhere)...........................	$_____	$_____
Life Insurance...	$_____	$_____
Savings/Investment..	$_____	$_____
Debt Service (from page 7) (not listed elsewhere)............	$_____	$_____
Parenting Time Expenses......................................	$_____	$_____
Professional Expenses (other than this proceeding)..........	$_____	$_____
Other (specify)...	$_____	$_____

*unreimbursed only...

TOTAL	$_____	$_____

Please Note: If you are paying expenses for a spouse and/or children not reflected in this budget, attach a schedule of such payments.

Schedule A: Shelter...	$_____	$_____
Schedule B: Transportation....................................	$_____	$_____
Schedule C: Personal...	$_____	$_____
Grand Totals...	$_____	$_____

153

PART E - BALANCE SHEET OF ALL FAMILY ASSETS AND LIABILITIES

STATEMENT OF ASSETS

Description	Title to Property (H, W, J)	Date of purchase/acquisition. If claim that asset is exempt, state reason and value of what is claimed to be exempt	Value $ Put * after exempt	Date of Evaluation Mo./Day/ Yr.
1. Real Property				
_____ _____		_____	_____	_____
2. Bank Accounts, CD's				
_____ _____		_____	_____	_____
_____ _____		_____	_____	_____
3. Vehicles				
_____ _____		_____	_____	_____
_____ _____		_____	_____	_____
_____ _____		_____	_____	_____
4. Tangible Personal Property				
_____ _____		_____	_____	_____
_____ _____		_____	_____	_____
_____ _____		_____	_____	_____
5. Stocks and Bonds				
_____ _____		_____	_____	_____
_____ _____		_____	_____	_____
_____ _____		_____	_____	_____
6. Pension, Profit Sharing, Retirement Plan(s) 40l(k)s, etc. [list each employer]				
_____ _____		_____	_____	_____
7. IRAs				
_____ _____		_____	_____	_____
_____ _____		_____	_____	_____
8. Businesses, Partnerships, Professional Practices				
_____ _____		_____	_____	_____
_____ _____		_____	_____	_____
9. Life Insurance (cash surrender value)				
_____ _____		_____	_____	_____
_____ _____		_____	_____	_____
10. Loans Receivable				
_____ _____		_____	_____	_____
_____ _____		_____	_____	_____
11. Other (specify)				
_____ _____		_____	_____	_____
_____ _____		_____	_____	_____

TOTAL GROSS ASSETS: $_____

TOTAL SUBJECT TO EQUITABLE DISTRIBUTION: $_____

TOTAL NOT SUBJECT TO EQUITABLE DISTRIBUTION: $_____

154

STATEMENT OF LIABILITIES

Description	Name of Responsible Party (H, W, J)	If you contend liability should not be considered in equitable distribution, state reason	Monthly Payment	Total Owed	Date
1. Real Estate Mortgages					
_____	_____	_____	_____	_____	_____
_____	_____	_____	_____	_____	_____
_____	_____	_____	_____	_____	_____
2. Other Long Term Debts					
_____	_____	_____	_____	_____	_____
_____	_____	_____	_____	_____	_____
_____	_____	_____	_____	_____	_____
3. Revolving Charges					
_____	_____	_____	_____	_____	_____
_____	_____	_____	_____	_____	_____
_____	_____	_____	_____	_____	_____
_____	_____	_____	_____	_____	_____
_____	_____	_____	_____	_____	_____
_____	_____	_____	_____	_____	_____
4. Other Short Term Debts					
_____	_____	_____	_____	_____	_____
_____	_____	_____	_____	_____	_____
_____	_____	_____	_____	_____	_____
5. Contingent Liabilities					
_____	_____	_____	_____	_____	_____
_____	_____	_____	_____	_____	_____

TOTAL GROSS LIABILITIES: $_____
(excluding contingent liabilities)

NET WORTH: $_____
(subject to equitable distribution)

PART F - STATEMENT OF SPECIAL PROBLEMS

Provide a Brief Narrative Statement of Any Special Problems Involving This Case: As example, state if the matter involves complex valuation problems (such as for a closely held business) or special medical problems of any family member etc.

I certify that the foregoing information contained herein is true. I am aware that if any of the foregoing information contained therein is willfully false, I am subject to punishment.

DATED: _____   SIGNED: _____

PART G - REQUIRED ATTACHMENTS

CHECK IF YOU HAVE ATTACHED THE FOLLOWING REQUIRED DOCUMENTS

1. A full and complete copy of your last federal and state income tax returns
   with all schedules and attachments. (Part C-1)   _____

2. Your last calendar year's W-2 statements, 1099's, K-1 statements.   _____

3. Your three most recent pay stubs.   _____

4. Bonus information including, but not limited to, percentage overrides, timing of payments, etc.;
   the last three statements of such bonuses, commissions, etc. (Part C)   _____

5. Your most recent corporate benefit statement or a summary thereof showing the nature, amount
   and status of retirement plans, savings plans, income deferral plans, insurance benefits, etc. (Part C)   _____

6. Affidavit of Insurance Coverage as required by Court Rule 5:4-2(f) (Part B-3)   _____

7. List of all prior/pending family actions involving support, custody or Domestic Violence, with the
   Docket Number, County, State and the disposition reached. Attach copies of all existing Orders in
   effect. (Part B-5)   _____

8. Attach details of each wage execution (Part C-5)

9. Schedule of payments made for a spouse and/or children not reflected in Part D.   _____

10. Any agreements between the parties.   _____

11. An Appendix IX Child Support Guideline Worksheet, as applicable, based upon available information.   _____

Confidential Litigant Information Sheet

To assure accuracy of court records
To be filled out by plaintiff or defendant or attorney
Collection of the following information is pursuant to N.J.S.A. 2A:17-56.60 and R. 5:7-4.
Confidentiality of this information must be maintained.

Docket #	**CS**

Your name _____
Last   First   Middle initial

Are you the **Plaintiff** or **Defendant**? (Circle one)	Social Security Number _____ - ___ - _____	Date of birth	Place of birth

Active Domestic Violence Order in this case? Yes or No. (Circle one)

Driver's license number, state of issuance

Your address	Your telephone number
Employer's name and address (or other income sources)	Telephone number
Professional, occupational, recreational licenses (types and numbers)	Your attorney's name and address

Health coverage for children (available through parent filling out this form)

Health care provider	Policy #	Group #
Dental care provider	Policy #	Group #
Prescription drug provider	Policy #	Group #

Children's information

Name (Last, first, middle initial)	Date of birth	Race	Sex	Social Security Number	Place of birth
1					
2					
3					
4					
5					
6					

Additional information (may be used to confirm identification if necessary)

Sex	Race	Height	Weight	Eyes	Hair	Complexion	Mustache?	Beard?

Glasses?	Tattoo (describe)	Auto license plate #, state of issuance	Car (model, make, year)

Mother's maiden name and address

Name _____
(Plaintiff's or defendant's name, address, and telephone number)

Address _____

_____

Telephone _____

_____, *Pro Se*
(Plaintiff or defendant)

SUPERIOR COURT OF NEW JERSEY
CHANCERY DIVISION—FAMILY PART

_____ COUNTY
(County where divorce complaint is filed)

DOCKET NO. _____
(Docket number of divorce case)

Name: _____
Plaintiff

vs.

Name: _____
Defendant

CIVIL ACTION

**REQUEST FOR
WAIVER OF FEES AND
SUPPORTING
CERTIFICATION**

Please enter an order granting _____ permission to waive
(Plaintiff or defendant)

the filing and service fees in this matter. The reasons for this request are set forth in the

certification attached below:

CERTIFICATION

I, _____, of full age, certify that:
(Your name)

1. I am the _____, *pro se* in the above-entitled action.
(Plaintiff or defendant)

2. I reside at _____
(Address of your residence)

_____.

3. I make this certification in support of my application for waiver of filing fees

and service fees pursuant to R. 1:13-2(a).

4. My net income is $ _____ per month derived from
(Your net monthly income)

_____. I have no
(The source[s] of your net monthly income)

other source of income.

5. The following is a true and complete listing of my assets to the best of my

knowledge, information, and belief:

    A. Bank accounts _____

    B. Automobiles _____

    C. Real estate _____

    D. Insurance with cash value _____

    E. Other _____

I have attached proof of my income to this certification in the form of copies

of the following documents:

_____

_____

_____

_____

I certify that the foregoing statements made by me are true. I am aware that if

any of the foregoing statements made by me are willfully false, I am subject to

punishment.

_____

(Plaintiff's or defendant's signature) Plaintiff or Defendant, *Pro Se*

_____

(Plaintiff's or defendant's name printed)

Dated _____

(Date on which you sign this document)

Name _____
      (Plaintiff's or defendant's name, address, and telephone number)

Address _____

_____

Telephone _____

_____, *Pro Se*
      (Plaintiff or defendant)

SUPERIOR COURT OF NEW JERSEY
CHANCERY DIVISION—FAMILY PART

_____ COUNTY
      (County where divorce complaint is filed)

DOCKET NO. FM _____
            (Docket number of divorce case)

_____

Name: _____
                  Plaintiff

            vs.

Name: _____
                  Defendant

_____

CIVIL ACTION

ORDER WAIVING FEES

The Court having examined the certification of _____,
                                                            (Your name)

_____, and it appearing that _____
      (Plaintiff or defendant)   (Plaintiff or defendant)

is a person of insufficient means to file this action in Court,

It is on this _____ day of _____ 20 ____ ,
                        (DO NOT WRITE HERE)

ORDERED that the request for a waiver of filing fees and service fees pursuant

to R. 1:13-2(a) is hereby granted.

_____, J.S.C.
            (DO NOT WRITE HERE)

Name _____
(Plaintiff's name, address, and telephone number)

Address _____

Telephone _____

Date_____

Plaintiff, *Pro Se*

Superior Court of New Jersey

_____ County, Family Part
(County where divorce complaint is filed)

_____
(Fill in address from Appendix A)

_____

_____, New Jersey, _____
(City)   (Zip code)

ATTENTION: FILING CLERK

RE: _____ Docket No. FM _____
(Caption/title of divorce case)   (Docket number of divorce case)

Dear Madam/Sir:

Enclosed please find an original and two copies of the following documents related to the above divorce matter:

(Place a check next to items enclosed)

___ 1. Complaint for divorce and attached certification of verification and non-collusion.

___ 2. Certification of insurance.

___ 3. Certification of notification of complementary dispute resolution.

___ 4. Request for waiver of fees and supporting certification.

___ 5. Form of order permitting waiver of fees.

___ 6. Family case information statement.

___ 7. Confidential litigant information sheet.

___ 8. Check or money order for Parents' Education Program fee. (If you have children)

___ 9. Check or money order for filing fee. (If your filing or service fees are not waived)

Kindly file the enclosed documents, retain the originals, and return two copies of each document marked "filed" in the enclosed self-addressed, stamped envelope.

Very truly yours,

_____
(Your signature)

Name _____
(Plaintiff's name, address, and telephone number)

Address _____

_____

Telephone _____

Plaintiff, *Pro Se*

SUPERIOR COURT OF NEW JERSEY
CHANCERY DIVISION—FAMILY PART

_____ COUNTY
(County where divorce complaint is filed)

DOCKET NO. FM _____
(Docket number of divorce complaint)

Name: _____
Plaintiff

vs.

Name: _____
Defendant

CIVIL ACTION

SUMMONS

FROM THE STATE OF NEW JERSEY
TO THE DEFENDANT NAMED ABOVE:

The plaintiff named above has filed a lawsuit against you in the Superior Court of New Jersey. The complaint attached to this summons states the basis for this lawsuit. If you dispute this complaint, you or your attorney must file either (1) a written answer or (2) a general appearance in accordance with R. 5:4-3(a) and proof of service with the

deputy clerk of the Superior Court, _____ County,
(County where divorce complaint was filed)

located at _____,
(Address of the Family Part of Superior Court in the county where divorce complaint was filed—see Appendix A)

New Jersey, within 35 days from the date you receive this summons, not counting the

date you receive it. A filing fee of _____ payable to the clerk of the
(Call the court for the filing fee)

Superior Court must accompany your answer or motion or appearance when it is filed.

You must also send a copy of your answer or motion or appearance to plaintiff's attorney, whose name and address appear above, or to plaintiff if no attorney is named above. A telephone call will not protect your rights; you must file and serve a written answer or motion (with fee and completed Case Information Statement) if you want the court to consider your answer or motion.

If you do not file and serve a written answer or motion or general appearance within 35 days, the court may enter a judgment against you for the relief plaintiff demands, plus interest and costs of the lawsuit. If judgment is entered against you, the Sheriff may seize your money, wages, or property to pay all or part of the judgment.

If you cannot afford an attorney, you may call the Legal Services office in the county where you live. A list of these offices is attached to this form. If you do not have an attorney and are not eligible for free legal assistance, you may obtain a referral to an attorney by calling one of the Lawyer Referral Services. A list of these numbers is also provided.

_____
(Sign the name "Theodore J. Fetter" and initial it with your initials)

Theodore J. Fetter
Acting Clerk, Superior Court

Date _____
(Date on which you sign the document)

_____

Name of defendant to be served _____
(Defendant's name)

Address of defendant to be served _____
(Defendant's address)

_____

Description of defendant to be served _____
(Physical description of the defendant)

_____

Best time to serve the defendant _____
(Day and time defendant is most likely to be at home)

COURT OFFICER'S PROOF OF SERVICE/RETURN OF SERVICE

(DO NOT FILL OUT THIS SECTION. This page will be filled out by the sheriff's officer and returned to the plaintiff.)

On _____, I, the undersigned, being

over the age of 18, served the within summons and complaint by delivering a copy

thereof to the person named therein at _____

_____.

I certify that the foregoing statements made by me are true. I am aware that if

any of the foregoing statements made by me are willfully false, I am subject to

punishment.

_____   _____
Signature   Date

_____

Docket No. _____

Date _____   Time _____

Height _____   Weight _____

Age _____   Hair _____

WM   WF   BM   BF   Other _____

Mustache   Beard   Glasses

Name _____

Relationship _____

Description of Premises _____

County Bar Association Lawyer Referral Services

Atlantic County Bar Association
NJ Lawyer Referral Service
Atlantic County Court House,
1201 Bacharach Blvd.
Atlantic City 08401
(609) 345-3444
Fax: (609) 345-6279
E-Mail: atcobara@aol.com

Bergen County Bar Association
NJ Lawyer Referral Service
15 Bergen Street
Hackensack 07601
(201) 488-0044
Fax: (201) 488-0073

**Burlington County Bar
Association**
NJ Lawyer Referral Service
45 Grant Street
Mount Holly 08060
(609) 261-4862
Fax: (609) 261-5423
Internet: www.burlcobar.org

**Camden County Bar
Association**
NJ Lawyer Referral Service
800 Cooper Street, Suite 103
Camden 08102
(856) 482-0618
Fax: (856) 482-0637
Internet:
www.camdencountybar.org

Cape May County
NJ Lawyer Referral Service
Rt. 9, Main Street
P.O. Box 425
Cape May Court House 08210
(609) 961-0172
Fax: (609) 778-1193
E-Mail:
CapeMayCtyBarAsn@aol.com

Cumberland County
NJ Lawyer Referral Service
P.O. Box 2031
Vineland 08362-2031
(856) 825-2001
Fax: (856) 692-2317

Essex County Bar Association
NJ Lawyer Referral Service
354 Eisenhower Parkway
Plaza 2
Livingston, NJ 07039
(973) 533-6775
Fax: (973) 533-6720

**Gloucester County Bar
Association**
NJ Lawyer Referral Service
Justice Complex
P.O. Box 338
Woodbury 08096
(856) 848-4589
Fax: (856) 384-9580

Hudson County Bar Association
NJ Lawyer Referral Service
583 Newark Avenue
Jersey City 07306
(201) 798-2727
Fax: (201) 798-1740

Hunterdon County
NJ Lawyer Referral Service
P.O. Box 573
Annandale 08801
(908) 735-2611
Fax: (908) 735-0305
E-mail:
suzannevrancken@yahoo.com

Mercer County Bar Association
NJ Lawyer Referral Service
1245 Whitehorse-Mercerville Road
Suite 420
Hamilton 08619-3894
(609) 585-6200
Fax: (609) 585-5537
E-mail: Francine@mercerbar.com
Internet: www.mercerbar.com

**Middlesex County Bar
Association**
NJ Lawyer Referral Service
87 Bayard Street
New Brunswick 08901
(732) 828-0053
E-mail: jcowles@mcbalaw.com

Monmouth Bar Association
NJ Lawyer Referral Service
Court House
Freehold 07728
(732) 431-5544
Fax: (732) 431-2843

Morris/Sussex Bar Association
NJ Lawyer Referral Service
28 Schuyler Place
Morristown 07960
(973) 267-5882
Fax: (973) 605-8325

Ocean County Bar Association
NJ Lawyer Referral Service
Courthouse, P.O. Box 381
Toms River 08753
(732) 240-3666
Fax: (732) 240-4907

Passaic County Bar Association
NJ Lawyer Referral Service
Courthouse, Hamilton Street
Paterson 07505
(973) 278-9223

Salem County Bar Association
NJ Lawyer Referral Service
(856) 935-5629

**Somerset County Bar
Association**
NJ Lawyer Referral Service
Courthouse, 20 N. Bridge Street
P.O. Box 1095
Somerville 08876
(908) 685-2323
Fax: (908) 685-9839

Union County Bar Association
NJ Lawyer Referral Service
Courthouse, 1st Floor
Elizabeth 07207
(908) 353-4715
Fax: (908) 354-8222

Warren County Bar Association
NJ Lawyer Referral Service
413 Second Street
Belvidere 07823
(908) 387-1835

New Jersey Legal Services Programs

State Coordinating Program
Legal Services of New Jersey
P.O. Box 1357
Edison, NJ 08818-1357
(732) 572-9100
www.LSNJ.org
LSNJ-LAW™ toll-free statewide legal hotline:
1-888-LSNJ-LAW (1-888-576-5529)
www.LSNJLAW.org

Regional Legal Services Programs

Central Jersey Legal Services
Mercer County ....(609) 695-6249
Middlesex County—New Brunswick ....(732) 249-7600
Middlesex County—Perth Amboy ....(732)-324-1613
Union County...(908) 354-4340

Essex-Newark Legal Services..(973) 624-4500

Legal Services of Northwest Jersey
Hunterdon County..(908) 782-7979
Morris County ....(973) 285-6911
Somerset County..(908) 231-0840
Sussex County...(973) 383-7400
Warren County...(908) 475-2010

Northeast New Jersey Legal Services
Bergen County ....(201) 487-2166
Hudson County ....(201) 792-6363
Passaic County..(973) 523-2900

Ocean-Monmouth Legal Services
Monmouth County—Freehold..(732) 866-0020
Monmouth County—Long Branch ....(732) 222-3338
Ocean County...(732) 341-2727

South Jersey Legal Services
Atlantic County..(609) 348-4200
Burlington County ....(609) 261-1088
Camden County ....(856) 964-2010
Cape May County ....(609) 465-3001
Centralized Intake ....(800) 496-4570
Consumer Law Unit...(856) 429-8291
Cumberland/Salem Counties ....(856) 451-0003
Gloucester County ....(856) 848-5360

Name _____
        (Plaintiff's name, address, and telephone number)

Address _____

_____

Telephone _____

Date _____

Plaintiff, *Pro Se*

_____ County Sheriff's Office
    (County where divorce complaint is filed)

_____
            (Fill in address from Appendix B)

_____

_____, New Jersey _____
                (City)   (Zip code)

RE: _____ Docket No. FM _____
          (Caption/title of divorce case)   (Docket number of divorce case)

Dear Madam/Sir:

Enclosed please find an original and one copy of a summons, complaint,

certification of insurance, certification of notification of complementary dispute

resolution, and _____
            (Fill in "order waiving fees," or "check [or money order] covering the fees for service of these documents")

to be served upon _____, the defendant named
                              (Defendant's name)

in this action.

Please serve a copy of each of the enclosed documents upon the defendant at the

address listed on the summons and return a proof of service in the enclosed self-

addressed, stamped envelope.

Very truly yours,

_____
                    (Your signature)   Plaintiff, *Pro Se*

Name _____
(Plaintiff's name, address, and telephone number)

Address _____

_____

Telephone _____

Date _____

Plaintiff, *Pro Se*

Superior Court of New Jersey

_____ County Family Part
(County where divorce complaint is filed)

_____
(Fill in address from Appendix A)

_____

_____, New Jersey _____
(City) (Zip code)

ATTENTION: FILING CLERK

RE: _____ Docket No. FM _____
(Caption/title of divorce case) (Docket number of divorce case)

Dear Madam/Sir:

Enclosed please find an original and two copies of the sheriff's proof of service in the above divorce matter.

Kindly file the enclosed documents, retain the original, and return two copies marked "filed" in the enclosed self-addressed, stamped envelope.

Very truly yours,

_____
(Your signature)

Name _____
<small>(Plaintiff's name, address, and telephone number)</small>

Address _____

_____

Telephone _____

Plaintiff, *Pro Se*

SUPERIOR COURT OF NEW JERSEY
CHANCERY DIVISION—FAMILY PART

_____ COUNTY
<small>(County where divorce complaint is filed)</small>

DOCKET NO. FM _____
<small>Docket number of divorce case)</small>

Name: _____ Plaintiff vs. Name: _____ Defendant	CIVIL ACTION **ACKNOWLEGMENT OF SERVICE OF SUMMONS AND COMPLAINT**

The undersigned hereby acknowledges service of a copy of the summons and complaint

on this _____ day of _____, 20_____.
<small>(DO NOT WRITE IN THIS SPACE. DEFENDANT MUST FILL IN THE DATE HE OR SHE SIGNS THE DOCUMENT.)</small>

_____
<small>(DO NOT WRITE IN THIS SPACE. DEFENDANT MUST SIGN HIS OR HER NAME.)</small>

Sworn to and subscribed

before me this   *day*

of   *, 20*   *.*

_____
Notary Public   <small>(DO NOT WRITE IN THIS SPACE. NOTARY MUST SIGN
ON DATE THAT THE DEFENDANT SIGNS THE DOCUMENT.)</small>

Name _____
(Plaintiff's name and address)

Address _____

_____

Date _____

Plaintiff, *Pro Se*

_____
(Name and address of defendant or defendant's attorney)

_____

_____

_____, New Jersey _____
            (City)   (Zip code)

RE: _____ Docket No. FM _____
        (Caption/title of divorce case)   (Docket number of divorce case)

Dear _____:
(Name of defendant or defendant's attorney)

      Enclosed please find a copy of a summons, complaint for divorce, certification of insurance, certification of notification of complementary dispute resolution, and acknowledgment of service in the above matter. Please sign the enclosed acknowledgment of service form in the presence of a notary and return the form to me in the enclosed self-addressed, stamped envelope.

Very truly yours,

_____
(Your signature)

Name _____

(Plaintiff's name, address, and telephone number)

Address _____

_____

Telephone _____

Date _____

Plaintiff, *Pro Se*

Superior Court of New Jersey

_____ County Family Part

(County where divorce complaint is filed)

_____

(Fill in address from Appendix A)

_____

_____, New Jersey _____

(City)   (Zip code)

ATTENTION: FILING CLERK

RE: _____ Docket No. FM _____

(Caption/title of divorce case)   (Docket number of divorce case)

Dear Madam/Sir:

Enclosed please find an original and two copies of an acknowledgment of service in the above matter. Kindly file the enclosed documents, retain the original, and return two copies marked "filed" in the enclosed self-addressed, stamped envelope.

Very truly yours,

_____

(Your signature)

171

Name _____
(Plaintiff's name and address)

Address _____

_____

_____

Date _____

Plaintiff, *Pro Se*

_____
(Name of person to whom you are inquiring about the defendant's whereabouts)

_____
(Address of person to whom you are inquiring about the defendant's whereabouts)

_____

_____, _____ _____
(City)   (State)   (Zip code)

RE: _____ Docket No. FM _____
(Caption/title of divorce case)   (Docket number of divorce case)

Dear _____:
(Name of the person to whom plaintiff is writing)

    Please be advised that I have filed a complaint for divorce against

_____, your _____. I write to request
(Defendant's name)   (Defendant's relationship to the person)

that you inform me about the home address of _____, if you
(Defendant's name)

know that information.

    I am trying to give notice to_____of the
(Defendant's name)

fact that I have filed a complaint for divorce against _____ in order that _____
(Him/her)   (He/she)

might appear or answer and defend this complaint. To assist you in promptly returning

your answer to me, I have enclosed a stamped, self-addressed envelope.

    Thank you for your assistance.

                    Very truly yours,

_____
(Plaintiff's signature)

Name _____
(Plaintiff's name and address)

Address _____

_____

Date _____

_____
(Name and address of State Motor Vehicle Commission or
Department where defendant last held a driver license)

_____

_____

_____, _____ _____
(City)   (State)   (Zip code)

RE: _____ Docket No. FM _____
(Caption/title of your divorce case)   (Docket number of divorce case)

Dear Madam/Sir:

Please be advised that I have filed a complaint for divorce against

_____. I write to request that you provide me with any
(Defendant's name)

information concerning the address of _____. To the best of my
(Defendant's name)

knowledge, _____ holds a driver license from the State of
(Defendant's name)

_____.
(State where defendant last held a driver license)

The object of my inquiry is to give notice to _____
(Defendant's name)

of the fact that I have filed a complaint for divorce against _____ in order that _____
(Him/her)   (He/she)

might appear or answer and defend this complaint.

Please provide me with any address that you may have for

_____. For your convenience, I am enclosing a stamped,
(Defendant's name)

self-addressed envelope. Thank you for your consideration of this request.

Very truly yours,

_____
(Plaintiff's signature)

Name _____
      (Plaintiff's name and address)

Address _____

_____

Date _____

Postmaster
United States Post Office

_____
(Post office address in town where defendant was last known to live)

_____

_____, _____ _____
       (City)   (State)   (Zip code)

RE: Freedom of Information Act Search

_____
            (Defendant's name)

    RE: _____ Docket No. FM _____
        (Caption/title of divorce case)   (Docket number of divorce case)

Dear Madam/Sir:

    I have filed a complaint for divorce against _____.
                                                        (Defendant's name)

Pursuant to the Freedom of Information Act, I request that you provide me with the last

forwarding address for _____.
                              (Defendant's name)

    The object of my inquiry is to give notice to _____ of the
                                                        (Defendant's name)

fact that I have filed a complaint for divorce against _____ in order that _____
                                                          (Him/her)   (He/she)

might appear or answer and defend this complaint.

    Please provide me with any address that you may have for

_____, regardless of whether or not it is expired.
       (Defendant's name)

I am enclosing the required search fee of $ _____, along with a stamped, self-

addressed envelope. Thank you for your consideration of this request.

                              Very truly yours,

                              _____
                                        (Plaintiff's signature)

Name _____
(Plaintiff's name and address)

Address _____

_____

_____

Date _____

Defense Manpower Data Center
Attention: Military Verification
1600 Wilson Boulevard, Suite 400
Arlington, Virginia 22209-2593

RE: Request for a Certificate of Military Service or Non-Service

RE: _____ Docket No. FM _____
(Caption/title of divorce case)   (Docket number of divorce case)

Dear Madam/Sir:

Please be advised that I have filed a complaint for divorce against

_____. The two objects of this inquiry are
(Defendant's name)

(1) to obtain a certificate of military service or non-service and (2) to give notice to

_____ of the fact that I have filed
(Defendant's name)

a complaint for divorce against _____ in order that _____ might appear or
(Him/her)   (He/she)

answer and defend this complaint.

Please return to me a certificate alongwith any address that you might have,

regardless of whether it is expired. I enclose a self-addressed, stamped envelope for this

purpose. Thank you for your consideration of this request.

Very truly yours,

_____
(Plaintiff's signature)

Name _____
(Plaintiff's name and address)

Address _____

_____

_____

Date _____

United States Army
Commander USA EREC
Attn: Locator
8899 East 56th Street
Fort Benjamin Harrison, IN 46249-5031

RE: Request for a Certificate of Military Service or Non-Service

RE: _____ Docket No. FM _____
(Caption/title of divorce case)   (Docket number of divorce case)

Dear Madam/Sir:

Please be advised that I have filed a complaint for divorce against

_____. The two objects of this inquiry are
(Defendant's name)

(1) to obtain a certificate of military service or non-service and (2) to give notice to

_____ of the fact that I have filed
(Defendant's name)

a complaint for divorce against _____ in order that _____ might appear or
(Him/her)   (He/she)

answer and defend this complaint.

Please return to me a certificate along with any address that you might have,

regardless of whether it is expired. I enclose a check payable to Finance Officer and a

self-addressed, stamped envelope for this purpose. Thank you for your consideration of

this request.

Very truly yours,

_____
(Plaintiff's signature)

Name _____
(Plaintiff's name and address)

Address _____

_____

_____

Date _____

United States Air Force
Worldwide Locator
HQ AFMPC/RMIQL
550 C Street West, Suite 50
Randolph Air Force Base, TX 78150-4752

RE: Request for a Certificate of Military Service or Non-Service

      RE: _____ Docket No. FM _____
          (Caption/title of divorce case)   (Docket number of divorce case)

Dear Madam/Sir:

      Please be advised that I have filed a complaint for divorce against

_____. The two objects of this inquiry are
(Defendant's name)

(1) to obtain a certificate of military service or non-service and (2) to give notice to

_____ of the fact that I have filed
(Defendant's name)

a complaint for divorce against _____ in order that _____ might appear or
                                (Him/her)   (He/she)

answer and defend this complaint.

      Please return to me a certificate along with any address that you might have,

regardless of whether it is expired. I enclose a check payable to the DAQ-DE and a self-

addressed, stamped envelope for this purpose. Thank you for your consideration of this

request.

                      Very truly yours,

                 _____
                         (Plaintiff's signature)

Name _____
(Plaintiff's name and address)

Address _____

_____

_____

Date _____

United States Navy
Naval Personnel Command
PERS 312F
5720 Integrity Drive
Millington, TN 38055-3120

RE: Request for a Certificate of Military Service or Non-Service

RE: _____ Docket No. FM _____
(Caption/title of divorce case)　　　　　　　　　　　(Docket number of divorce case)

Dear Madam/Sir:

Please be advised that I have filed a complaint for divorce against

_____. The two objects of this inquiry are
(Defendant's name)

(1) to obtain a certificate of military service or non-service and (2) to give notice to

_____ of the fact that I have filed
(Defendant's name)

a complaint for divorce against _____ in order that _____ might appear or
　　　　　　　　　　　　　　　　　(Him/her)　　　　　　　　(He/she)

answer and defend this complaint.

Please return to me a certificate along with any address that you might have,

regardless of whether it is expired. I enclose a check payable to the United States

Treasurer and a self-addressed, stamped envelope for this purpose. Thank you for your

consideration of this request.

Very truly yours,

_____
(Plaintiff's signature)

Name _____
(Plaintiff's name and address)

Address _____

_____

_____

Date _____

United States Marine Corps
Headquarters, U.S. Marine Corps
Code MMSB10
Support BRMMSB 10, Suite 201
2008 Elliott Road, Suite 203
Quantico, VA 22134-5030

RE: Request for a Certificate of Military Service or Non-Service

RE: _____ Docket No. FM _____
(Caption/title of divorce case)   (Docket number of divorce case)

Dear Madam/Sir:

Please be advised that I have filed a complaint for divorce against

_____. The two objects of this inquiry are
(Defendant's name)

(1) to obtain a certificate of military service or non-service and (2) to give notice to

_____ of the fact that I have filed
(Defendant's name)

a complaint for divorce against _____ in order that _____ might appear or
(Him/her)   (He/she)

answer and defend this complaint.

Please return to me a certificate along with any address that you might have,

regardless of whether it is expired. I enclose a check payable to the United

States Treasurer and a self-addressed, stamped envelope for this purpose. Thank you for

your consideration of this request.

Very truly yours,

_____
(Plaintiff's signature)

Name _____
(Plaintiff's name and address)

Address _____

_____

_____

Date _____

United States Coast Guard
USCG—Personnel Command
2100 Second Street, S.W.
Washington, DC 20593-0001
Attn: Coast Guard Locator Assistant

RE: Request for a Certificate of Military Service or Non-Service

RE: _____ Docket No. FM _____
(Caption/title of divorce case)   (Docket number of divorce case)

Dear Madam/Sir:

Please be advised that I have filed a complaint for divorce against

_____. The two objects of this inquiry are
(Defendant's name)

(1) to obtain a certificate of military service or non-service and (2) to give notice to

_____ of the fact that I have filed
(Defendant's name)

a complaint for divorce against _____ in order that _____ might appear or
(Him/her)   (He/she)

answer and defend this complaint.

Please return to me a certificate along with any address that you might have,

regardless of whether it is expired. I enclose a check payable to the U.S. Coast Guard and

a self-addressed, stamped envelope for this purpose. Thank you for your consideration of

this request.

Very truly yours,

_____
(Plaintiff's signature)

180

Name _____
(Plaintiff's name, address, and telephone number)

Address _____

_____

Telephone _____

Plaintiff, *Pro Se*

SUPERIOR COURT OF NEW JERSEY
CHANCERY DIVISION—FAMILY PART

_____ COUNTY
(County where divorce complaint is filed)

DOCKET NO. FM _____
(Docket number of divorce case)

Name:_____

Plaintiff

vs.

Name:_____

Defendant

CIVIL ACTION

REQUEST FOR ORDER PERMITTING SUBSTITUTED SERVICE ON A SPECIAL AGENT AND SUPPORTING CERTIFICATION

Please enter an order granting plaintiff _____
(Your name)

permission to serve _____, the
(Defendant's name)

defendant in the above-entitled action, by way of substituted service upon

_____. The reasons
(Name of person accepting service on behalf of defendant)

for this request are set forth in the CERTIFICATION below:

CERTIFICATION

I, _____, of full age, certify that:
(Your name)

1. I am the plaintiff in the above-entitled action.

2. I do not know the present whereabouts of the defendant and have not seen or

heard from _____ directly or indirectly since on or about _____.
(Him/her)   (Date)

3. I have made diligent inquiry in good faith respecting the defendant's residency and post office address in an attempt to locate and serve defendant with the complaint in this matter.

4. More specifically, I have contacted the following individuals in an attempt to locate the defendant:

A. On or about _____, I

(Date)

_____

(Describe what you did in your attempt to locate the defendant. If you
sent a letter, say, "A copy of the letter is attached hereto as Exhibit A.")

_____.

B. On or about _____, I

(Date)

_____

(Describe what you did in your attempt to locate the defendant. If you
sent a letter, say, "A copy of the letter is attached hereto as Exhibit B.")

_____.

5. In further attempts to locate the defendant, I did the following:

(Fill in the applicable sections)

A. I obtained a motor vehicle search from

_____.

(Title of the State Motor Vehicles Commission or Division where you requested the search)

They had no information as to the defendant's whereabouts. A copy of this search is attached hereto as Exhibit _____.

B. I checked all of the telephone books for _____,

(County)

_____, _____, and _____

(County)   (County)   (County)

counties, and did not find the name of the defendant listed therein.

C. I have telephoned defendant's employer

_____,

(Name of defendant's employer)

and this employer does not know defendant's whereabouts.

D. I have written to the post office in town and they indicated through a written reply that there is no forwarding address for defendant.

A copy of this reply is attached hereto as Exhibit D.

6. To the best of my knowledge, I know of no individuals other than

_____, defendant's _____,
(Name of person to be served)   (Relationship to defendant)

who lives at _____
(Address of person to be served)

_____,

with whom defendant might be residing or communicating.

7. I do not know of any other person connected with the defendant by marriage

or business who knows defendant's residence or post office address.

8. I believe that service cannot be made within this state or outside of this state in

the manner prescribed by paragraphs (a) or (b) of R. 4:4-5 of this Court, and therefore

apply for an order for substituted service under paragraph (d) of that Rule, or for

another form of service as the Court shall deem proper.

9. For the reasons set forth above, I request that the Court order substituted

service upon _____, the defendant's _____,
(Name of person to be served)   (Relationship to defendant)

at _____ residence at _____
(His/her)   (Address of person to be served)

_____.

I certify that the foregoing statements made by me are true. I am aware that if

any of the foregoing statements made by me are willfully false, I am subject to

punishment.

_____
(Your signature)   Plaintiff, *Pro Se*

_____
(Your name printed)

Dated _____
(Date on which you sign this document)

Name _____
(Plaintiff's name, address, and telephone number)

Address _____

_____

Telephone _____

Plaintiff, *Pro Se*

SUPERIOR COURT OF NEW JERSEY
CHANCERY DIVISION—FAMILY PART

_____ COUNTY
(County where divorce complaint is filed)

DOCKET NO. FM _____
(Docket number of divorce case)

Name: _____ Plaintiff vs. Name: _____ Defendant	CIVIL ACTION **ORDER PERMITTING** **SUBSTITUTED** **SERVICE ON A** **SPECIAL AGENT**

THIS MATTER having come to the attention of the Court by way of plaintiff's application, and it appearing upon a review of the certification of the plaintiff that service of process cannot be effected within the State of New Jersey; and it further appearing that after diligent inquiry and effort, defendant's whereabouts are unknown; and it further appearing that _____,
(Name of person to be served)

located at _____
(Address of person to be served)

_____

is the only person who may be served in place of the defendant, and the Court having considered same and for good cause shown;

It is on this _____ day of _____, 20_____
(DO NOT WRITE HERE)

ORDERED as follows:

That the defendant shall file with the Court and serve upon plaintiff, whose

name and address appear above, either

(1) A written appearance in accordance with Rule 5:4-3(a), or

(2) An answer to the complaint, on or before the _____
(DO NOT WRITE HERE)

day of _____, 20_____; and that if the defendant
(DO NOT WRITE HERE)

fails to file an answer or a written appearance in accordance with

R. 5:4-3(a), judgment by default may be rendered against the defendant

for the relief demanded in the complaint, and it is

FURTHER ORDERED:

(1) That if the defendant is unable to obtain an attorney, the

defendant may contact the lawyer referral service of the county of

_____ by calling _____,
(County where divorce complaint is filed) (Telephone number of lawyer referral service—
see Appendix C)

and further that if the defendant cannot afford an attorney, the defendant

may contact _____
(Regional Legal Services office serving county where divorce complaint is filed)

by calling _____;
(Telephone number of Legal Services office—see Appendix D)

(2) That the defendant shall promptly file the answer or written

appearance and proof of service thereof in duplicate with the clerk of

the Superior Court, _____ County,
(County where divorce complaint is filed)

at _____,
(Address of Superior Court, Family Part, in county where divorce complaint is filed—see
Appendix A)

_____

in accordance with the rules of civil practice and procedure; and it is

FURTHER ORDERED:

(1) That substituted service upon a special agent shall replace personal service upon the defendant of the complaint and notice of the within order, and that this substituted service shall be made no later than

_____ upon
(DO NOT WRITE HERE)

_____at _____ residence
(Name of person to be served)   (His/her)

at _____
(Address of person to be served)

_____

personally or by leaving a copy thereof at _____ dwelling, house, or
(His/her)

usual place of abode with a competent member of _____ household of
(His/her)

the age of 14 years or older then residing therein, or by registered or certified mail, return receipt requested, but if the addressee refuses to claim or accept delivery of said registered or certified mail, then by ordinary mail, and proof of service shall be filed.

_____
(DO NOT WRITE HERE)   J.S.C.

Name _____
(Plaintiff's name, address, and telephone number)

Address _____

_____

Telephone _____

Date _____

Plaintiff, *Pro Se*

Superior Court of New Jersey

_____ County, Family Part
(County where divorce complaint is filed)

_____
(Fill in address from Appendix A)

_____

_____, New Jersey _____
(City)   (Zip code)

ATTENTION: FILING CLERK

RE: _____ Docket No. FM _____
(Caption/title of divorce case)   (Docket number of divorce case)

Dear Madam/Sir:

Enclosed please find an original and two copies of a request for permission to serve defendant by substituted service and supporting certification and a form of order permitting substituted service in the above matter.

Kindly file the enclosed documents, retain the original, and return two copies marked "filed" in the enclosed self-addressed, stamped envelope.

Very truly yours,

_____
(Your signature)

187

Name _____
(Plaintiff's name, address, and telephone number)

Address _____

_____

Telephone _____

Plaintiff, *Pro Se*

SUPERIOR COURT OF NEW JERSEY
CHANCERY DIVISION—FAMILY PART

_____ COUNTY
(County where divorce complaint is filed)

DOCKET NO. FM _____
(Docket number of divorce case)

Name: _____ Plaintiff vs. Name: _____ Defendant	CIVIL ACTION **REQUEST FOR ORDER PERMITTING SERVICE BY PUBLICATION AND SUPPORTING CERTIFICATION**

Please enter an order granting plaintiff _____
(Plaintiff's name)

permission to serve _____, the defendant in the
(Defendant's name)

above-entitled action, by way of publication. The reasons for this request are set forth in

the CERTIFICATION below:

CERTIFICATION

I, _____, of full age, certify that:
(Plaintiff's name)

1. I am the plaintiff in the above-entitled action.

2. I do not know the present whereabouts of the defendant and have not seen or

heard from _____ directly or indirectly since on or about _____.
(Him/her)   (Date)

3. I have made diligent inquiry in good faith respecting the defendant's residency, post office address, and occupation, in an attempt to locate and serve defendant with the complaint in this matter.

4. More specifically, I have attempted to contact the following individuals in an attempt to locate the defendant:

A. On or about _____, I
(Date)

_____
(Describe what you did in your attempt to locate the defendant. If you
sent a letter, say, "A copy of the letter is attached hereto as Exhibit A.")

_____

B. On or about _____, I
(Date)

_____
(Describe what you did in your attempt to locate the defendant. If you
sent a letter, say, "A copy of the letter is attached hereto as Exhibit B.")

_____

5. In further attempts to locate the defendant, I did the following:

(Check the applicable sections)

___ A. I have obtained a motor vehicle search from the

_____.
(Title of the State Motor Vehicle Commission or Division where you requested the search)

They had no information as to defendant's whereabouts. A copy of this search is attached hereto as Exhibit _____.

___ B. I have checked all of the telephone books for _____,
(County)

_____, _____, and _____
(County)   (County)   (County)

counties, and did not find the name of the defendant listed therein.

___ C. I have telephoned defendant's employer,

_____
(Name of defendant's employer)

and this employer does not know defendant's whereabouts.

___ D. I have written to _____
(Postmaster to whom you inquired about defendant's forwarding address)

and the postmaster indicated through a written reply that there is no

forwarding address for defendant. A copy of this reply is attached hereto as

Exhibit _____.

6. To the best of my knowledge, I know of no other individuals with whom

defendant might be residing or communicating.

7. I do not know of any other person connected with the defendant by marriage,

or in business, or of any person whom I have reason to believe has knowledge of the

residence or post office address of the defendant.

8. I believe that the defendant is not a resident of this state and cannot be

found in this state, and that process cannot be served upon _____ within or without of
(Him/her)

the state in the manner prescribed by paragraphs (a) or (b) of R. 4:4-5, and I cannot

suggest any other special form of substituted service under the Rules that would be likely

to give actual notice of this suit to the defendant.

9. For the reasons set forth above, I request that the Court order publication in

the _____,
(Name of newspaper in the county where divorce complaint is filed)

a newspaper with circulation in _____County.
(County where divorce complaint is filed)

I certify that the foregoing statements made by me are true. I am aware that if any

of the foregoing statements made by me are willfully false, I am subject to punishment.

_____
(Your signature)   Plaintiff, *Pro Se*

_____
(Your name printed)

Dated _____
(Date on which you sign this document)

Name _____
(Plaintiff's name, address, and telephone number)

Address _____

_____

Telephone _____

Plaintiff, *Pro Se*

SUPERIOR COURT OF NEW JERSEY
CHANCERY DIVISION—FAMILY PART

_____ COUNTY
(County where divorce complaint is filed)

DOCKET NO. FM _____
(Docket number of divorce case)

Name: _____ Plaintiff vs. Name: _____ Defendant	CIVIL ACTION **ORDER PERMITTING SERVICE BY PUBLICATION**

THIS MATTER having come to the attention of the Court by way of plaintiff's application, and it appearing upon a review of the certification of the plaintiff that service of process cannot be effected within the State of New Jersey, and it further appearing that after diligent inquiry and effort, defendant's whereabouts are unknown; and it further appearing that there is no person who may be served in place of the defendant, and the Court having considered same and for good cause shown;

It is on this _____ day of _____, 20_____,
(D O N O T W R I T E H E R E)

ORDERED as follows:

Within _____ days of the date of this order, plaintiff shall
(DO NOT WRITE HERE)

file a notice of the filing of the divorce complaint in the

_____,
(Name of newspaper in the county where the divorce complaint is filed)

a newspaper with circulation in _____ County.
(County where divorce complaint is filed)

It is FURTHER ORDERED:

That proof of publication by way of affidavit of publication from said

newspaper shall be filed with the Court within _____ days
(DO NOT WRITE HERE)

of the date of said affidavit, and it is

FURTHER ORDERED:

That within _____ days of the date of filing of the
(DO NOT WRITE HERE)

affidavit of publication with the Court, the defendant shall serve upon plaintiff,

whose name and address appear above, either

(1) A written appearance in accordance with R. 5:4-3(a), or

(2) An answer to the complaint, on or before the _____ day of
(DO NOT WRITE HERE)

_____, 20_____, and that if defendant fails to
(DO NOT WRITE HERE)

answer or file a written appearance in accordance with R. 5:4-3(a), judgment

by default may be rendered against the defendant for the relief demanded in the

complaint, and it is

FURTHER ORDERED:

(1) That if the defendant is unable to obtain an attorney, that the defendant may

contact the lawyer referral service of the county of _____,
(County where the divorce complaint is filed)

by calling _____, and further that if the defendant
(Telephone number of lawyer referral service—see Appendix C)

cannot afford an attorney, the defendant may contact _____
(Regional Legal Services office serving county where divorce complaint is filed)

_____ by calling _____;
(Telephone number of Legal Services office—see Appendix D)

(2) That the defendant shall promptly file the answer or written

appearance and proof of service thereof in duplicate with the Clerk of

the Superior Court, _____ County, at
(County where divorce complaint is filed)

_____, in
(Address of Superior Court, Family Part, in county where divorce complaint is filed—see Appendix A)

accordance with the rules of civil practice and procedure.

_____
(DO NOT WRITE HERE)   J.S.C.

Name _____
(Plaintiff's name, address, and telephone number)

Address _____

_____

Telephone _____

Date _____

Plaintiff, *Pro Se*

Superior Court of New Jersey

_____ County Family Part
(County where divorce complaint is filed)

_____
(Fill in address from Appendix A)

_____

_____, New Jersey _____
(City)   (Zip code)

ATTENTION: FILING CLERK

RE: _____ Docket No. FM _____
(Caption/title of divorce case)   (Docket number of divorce case)

Dear Madam/Sir:

Enclosed please find an original and two copies of a request for permission to serve defendant by publication and supporting certification and a form of order permitting service by publication in the above matter.

Kindly file the enclosed documents, retain the original, and return two copies marked "filed" in the enclosed self-addressed, stamped envelope.

Very truly yours,

_____
(Your signature)

SUPERIOR COURT OF NEW JERSEY
CHANCERY DIVISION, FAMILY PART

_____ COUNTY
(County where divorce complaint is filed)

DOCKET NO. FM _____
(Docket number of divorce case)

TO _____
(Defendant's full name in upper-case letters)

By order of the Superior Court of New Jersey, wherein

_____ is the plaintiff,
(Plaintiff's name)

and you, _____ _____, are the defendant, you are required to serve upon the
(His/her)   (Husband/wife)

plaintiff, _____, _____
(Plaintiff's name)   (Plaintiff's address)

_____, either

(1) a written appearance in accordance with R. 5:4-3(a), or (2) an answer to the

complaint, on or before the _____ day of _____, 20_____,
(DO NOT WRITE HERE)

and if you fail to answer or file a written appearance in accordance with R. 5:4-3(a),

judgment by default may be rendered against you for the relief demanded in the

complaint; and further, you shall promptly file the answer or written appearance and

proof of service thereof in duplicate with the matrimonial filing clerk in the Superior

Court, _____, located at _____
(County where divorce complaint is filed)   (See Appendix A for address of the Superior Court, Family Part)

_____, in accordance with the Rules of

Civil Practice and Procedure.

The telephone numbers for assistance in obtaining an attorney in the county in

which this action is pending are:

Lawyer referral service _____
(See Appendix C for lawyer referral services telephone numbers)

Legal Services office _____
(See Appendix D for telephone numbers of New Jersey Legal Services offices)

195

Name _____
(Plaintiff's name, address, and telephone number)

Address _____

_____

Telephone _____

Date _____

Plaintiff, *Pro Se*

_____
(Name of newspaper ordered by court to publish notice)

_____
(Address of newspaper)

_____

_____, _____ _____
(City)   (State)   (Zip code)

_____
(Country)

RE: _____ Docket No. FM _____
(Caption/title of divorce case)   (Docket number of divorce case)

Dear Madam/Sir:

Enclosed please find a notice of order for publication from the Superior Court of New Jersey, which directs that you publish this notice in your newspaper for a period of

_____.
(Length of time ordered in order permitting service by publication)

Very truly yours,

_____
(Your signature)

196

Name_____
(Plaintiff's name, address, and telephone number)

Address_____

_____

Telephone_____

Date_____

Plaintiff, *Pro Se*

Superior Court of New Jersey

_____ County Family Part
(County where divorce complaint is filed)

_____
(Fill in address from Appendix A)

_____

_____, New Jersey _____
(City)   (Zip code)

ATTENTION: FILING CLERK

RE: _____ Docket No. FM _____
(Caption/title of divorce case)   (Docket number of divorce case)

Dear Madam/Sir:

Enclosed please find an original and two copies of the certification of publication

of the _____
(Name of the newspaper)

in the above matter. Kindly file this document, and return two copies marked "filed" in

the enclosed self-addressed, stamped envelope.

Very truly yours,

_____
(Your signature)

Name _____
(Defendant's name, address, and telephone number)

Address _____

_____

Telephone _____

Defendant, *Pro Se*

SUPERIOR COURT OF NEW JERSEY
CHANCERY DIVISION—FAMILY PART

_____ COUNTY
(County where divorce complaint is filed)

DOCKET NO. FM _____
(Docket number of divorce case)

Name: _____
Plaintiff

vs.

Name: _____
Defendant

CIVIL ACTION

**CONSENT ORDER
EXTENDING TIME
TO ANSWER**

THIS MATTER being opened to the Court by _____
(Defendant or counsel for defendant)

and with the consent of plaintiff, and it appearing to the Court that the parties have

agreed to the entry of this order and for good cause shown;

It is on this _____ day of _____, 20_____,
(DO NOT WRITE HERE)

ORDERED:

1. The defendant shall respond to the complaint of the plaintiff in the within

action on or before _____ (date not to exceed
(DO NOT WRITE HERE)

60 days from the original date on which the answer was due).

198

2. A copy of this order shall be served on all parties within seven (7) days of the date of this order.

_____
(DO NOT WRITE HERE)   J.S.C.

We hereby consent to the form and entry of this order.

_____
(Defendant's or defendant's attorney's signature)

_____
(Defendant's or defendant's attorney's name, typed or printed)

Date _____
(Date on which you sign this document)

_____
(Plaintiff's or plaintiff's attorney's signature)

_____
(Plaintiff's or plaintiff's attorney's name, typed or printed)

Date _____
(Date on which you sign this document)

Name _____
(Defendant's name, address, and telephone number)

Address _____

_____

Telephone _____

Date _____

Defendant, *Pro Se*

Superior Court of New Jersey

_____ County Family Part
(County where divorce complaint is filed)

_____
(Fill in address from Appendix A)

_____

_____, New Jersey _____
(City) (Zip code)

ATTENTION: FILING CLERK

RE: _____ Docket No. FM _____
(Caption/title of divorce case) (Docket number of divorce case)

Dear Madam/Sir:

Enclosed please find an original and two copies of a consent order extending time to answer in the above divorce matter. Kindly file the enclosed documents, retain the original, and return two copies marked "filed" in the enclosed self-addressed, stamped envelope.

Very truly yours,

_____
(Your signature)

Name _____
(Defendant's name, address, and telephone number)

Address _____

_____

Telephone _____

Defendant, *Pro Se*

SUPERIOR COURT OF NEW JERSEY
CHANCERY DIVISION—FAMILY PART

_____ COUNTY
(County where divorce complaint is filed)

DOCKET NO. FM _____
(Docket number of divorce case)

Name: _____
Plaintiff

vs.

Name: _____
Defendant

CIVIL ACTION

**ANSWER AND
COUNTERCLAIM
FOR DIVORCE
Based on Separation**

The defendant, _____, residing at
(Defendant's name)

_____,
(Defendant's address)

_____ County, State of _____, by way of answer to the

plaintiff's complaint says:

1. I _____ the allegations contained in paragraph 1.
   (Admit/deny)

2. I _____ the allegations contained in paragraph 2.
   (Admit/deny)

3. I _____ the allegations contained in paragraph 3.
   (Admit/deny)

4. I _____ the allegations contained in paragraph 4.
   (Admit/deny)

201

5. I _____ the allegations contained in paragraph 5.
    _____(Admit/deny)_____

6. I _____ the allegations contained in paragraph 6.
    _____(Admit/deny)_____

7. I _____ the allegations contained in paragraph 7.
    _____(Admit/deny)_____

8. I _____ the allegations contained in paragraph 8.
    _____(Admit/deny)_____

WHEREFORE, defendant demands judgment dismissing plaintiff's complaint together with interests and costs of suit.

COUNTERCLAIM FOR DIVORCE
Based on Separation

1. The defendant was lawfully married to _____,
    _____(Plaintiff's name)_____

the plaintiff herein, on _____ in a _____
    _____(Date of the marriage)_____   _____(Type of ceremony)_____

ceremony performed by _____.
    _____(Name of the person who performed the ceremony)_____

2. The parties separated on or about _____.
    _____(Date on which you and plaintiff began to live in separate locations)_____

Ever since that time and for 18 consecutive months, the parties have lived separate and apart and in different locations. The separation has continued to the present time, and there is no reasonable prospect of reconciliation.

3. At the point at which defendant and plaintiff had lived separately for at least 18 months, defendant was a *bona fide* resident of the State of New Jersey. Since that date, and for more than one year before the date of filing of this complaint, defendant has continued to be a *bona fide* resident of this state.

4. At the point at which defendant and plaintiff had lived separately for at least 18 months, defendant lived at _____

_____,
    _____(Defendant's address at the time the defendant had been separated from plaintiff for 18 months)_____

City of _____, County of _____, and

State of _____.

5. The plaintiff, _____, resides at
(Plaintiff's name)

_____
(Plaintiff's address)

_____.

6. (Check the appropriate statement below and fill in information where applicable)

    ____ A. No children were born of this marriage.

    ____ B. The following children were born of this marriage:

_____	_____
(Name)	(Birth date)
(Name)	(Birth date)
(Name)	(Birth date)
(Name)	(Birth date)

    ____C. An order for child support was entered on _____
(Date of original order)

under docket number _____.
(Docket number of child support case)

7. The plaintiff and defendant in the matter within have been parties to the

following prior actions:

(List any other court cases where you or your spouse are involved in a lawsuit, such as cases for bankruptcy, personal injury, child support, custody, domestic violence, etc.)

    A. _____ _____
        (Caption or title of case)   (Docket number)

    B. _____ _____
        (Caption or title of case)   (Docket number)

    C. _____ _____
        (Caption or title of case)   (Docket number)

    D. _____ _____
        (Caption or title of case)   (Docket number)

WHEREFORE, defendant demands judgment:

(Check the appropriate statement below and fill in information where applicable)

    ____ A. Dissolving the marriage between the parties;

____ B. Ordering that all debts and assets be equitably distributed between the

parties;

____ C. Ordering that plaintiff pay child support to defendant;

____ D. Ordering that defendant have physical custody of/be the parent of

primary custody for the minor children of the marriage;

____ E. Ordering that plaintiff pay alimony to defendant;

____ F. Permitting defendant to assume the use of the name of

_____;
(The name that you would like to assume after your divorce)

____ G. Granting such further relief as the Court may deem just and equitable.

_____
(Defendant's signature)

_____
(Defendant's name printed)   Defendant, *Pro Se*

Dated _____
(Date on which defendant signs this document)

.

CERTIFICATION OF VERIFICATION AND NON-COLLUSION PURSUANT TO R. 4:5-1

1. I am the defendant in the foregoing counterclaim.

2. The allegations of the counterclaim are true to the best of my knowledge, information, and belief. The counterclaim is made in truth and good faith and without collusion for the causes set forth therein.

3. The matter in controversy in the within action is not the subject of any other action pending in any court or of a pending arbitration proceeding, nor is any such court action or arbitration proceeding presently contemplated. There are no other persons who should be joined in this action at this time.

I certify that the foregoing statements made by me are true. I am aware that if any of the foregoing statements made by me are willfully false, I am subject to punishment.

_____
(Defendant's signature) Defendant, *Pro Se*

_____
(Defendant's name printed)

Dated _____
(Date on which defendant signs this document)

The undersigned hereby certifies that this pleading was served within the time permitted by the New Jersey Court Rules.

_____
(Defendant's signature) Defendant, *Pro Se*

Name _____
(Defendant's name, address, and telephone number)

Address _____

_____

Telephone _____

Defendant, *Pro Se*

SUPERIOR COURT OF NEW JERSEY
CHANCERY DIVISION—FAMILY PART

_____ COUNTY
(County where divorce complaint is filed)

DOCKET NO. FM _____
(Docket number of divorce case)

Name: _____
Plaintiff

vs.

Name: _____
Defendant

CIVIL ACTION

ANSWER AND COUNTERCLAIM FOR DIVORCE Based on Desertion

The defendant, _____, residing at
(Defendant's name)

_____,
(Defendant's address)

_____ County, State of _____, by way of answer to the

plaintiff's complaint says:

1. I _____ the allegations contained in paragraph 1.
(Admit/deny)

2. I _____ the allegations contained in paragraph 2.
(Admit/deny)

3. I _____ the allegations contained in paragraph 3.
(Admit/deny)

4. I _____ the allegations contained in paragraph 4.
(Admit/deny)

5. I _____ the allegations contained in paragraph 5.
       (Admit/deny)

6. I _____ the allegations contained in paragraph 6.
       (Admit/deny)

7. I _____ the allegations contained in paragraph 7.
       (Admit/deny)

8. I _____ the allegations contained in paragraph 8.
       (Admit/deny)

WHEREFORE, defendant demands judgment dismissing plaintiff's complaint together with interests and costs of suit.

COUNTERCLAIM FOR DIVORCE
Based on Desertion

1. The defendant was lawfully married to _____,
                                              (Plaintiff's name)
the plaintiff herein, on _____ in a _____
                              (Date of the marriage)   (Type of ceremony)
ceremony performed by _____.
                              (Name of the person who performed the ceremony)

2. The plaintiff deserted the defendant on or about _____,
                                                          (Date on which plaintiff deserted you)
ever since which time and for more than 12 consecutive months, plaintiff has willfully and continuously deserted the defendant.

3. At the point at which plaintiff had deserted defendant for 12 consecutive months, defendant was a *bona fide* resident of the State of New Jersey. Since that date, and for more than one year before the date of filing of this counterclaim, defendant has continued to be a *bona fide* resident of this state.

4. At the point at which plaintiff had deserted defendant for 12 consecutive months, defendant lived at _____
                       (Defendant's address at the time that plaintiff had deserted him/her for 12 months)
_____, City of _____, County of _____,
State of New Jersey.

5. The plaintiff, _____, resides at

(Plaintiff's name)

_____

(Plaintiff's address)

_____.

6. (Check the appropriate statement below and fill in information where applicable)

____ A. No children were born of this marriage.

____ B. The following children were born of this marriage:

_____	_____
(Name)	(Birth date)
_____	_____
(Name)	(Birth date)
_____	_____
(Name)	(Birth date)
_____	_____
(Name)	(Birth date)

____ C. An order for child support was entered on _____

(Date of original order)

under docket number _____.

(Docket number of child support case)

7. The plaintiff and defendant in the matter within have been parties to the

following prior actions:

(List any other court cases where you or your spouse are involved in a lawsuit, such as cases for bankruptcy, personal injury, child support, custody, domestic violence, etc.)

A. _____ _____

(Caption or title of case) (Docket number)

B. _____ _____

(Caption or title of case) (Docket number)

C. _____ _____

(Caption or title of case) (Docket number)

D. _____ _____

(Caption or title of case) (Docket number)

WHEREFORE, defendant demands judgment:

(Check the appropriate statement below and fill in information where applicable)

____ A. Dissolving the marriage between the parties;

_____ B. Ordering that all debts and assets be equitably distributed between the

parties;

_____ C. Ordering that plaintiff pay child support to defendant;

_____ D. Ordering that defendant have physical custody of/be the parent of

primary custody for the minor children of the marriage;

_____ E. Ordering that plaintiff pay alimony to defendant;

_____ F. Permitting defendant to assume the use of the name of

_____;
(The name that you would like to assume after your divorce)

_____ G. Granting such further relief as the Court may deem just and equitable.

_____
(Defendant's signature)

_____
(Defendant's name printed) Defendant, Pro Se

Dated _____
(Date on which defendant signs this document)

CERTIFICATION OF VERIFICATION AND NON-COLLUSION PURSUANT TO R. 4:5-1

1. I am the defendant in the foregoing counterclaim.

2. The allegations of the counterclaim are true to the best of my knowledge, information and belief. The counterclaim is made in truth and good faith and without collusion for the causes set forth therein.

3. The matter in controversy in the within action is not the subject of any other action pending in any court or of a pending arbitration proceeding, nor is any such court action or arbitration proceeding presently contemplated. There are no other persons who should be joined in this action at this time.

I certify that the foregoing statements made by me are true. I am aware that if any of the foregoing statements made by me are willfully false, I am subject to punishment.

_____
(Defendant's signature)   Defendant, *Pro Se*

_____
(Defendant's name printed)

Dated _____
      (Date on which defendant signs this document)

The undersigned hereby certifies that this pleading was served within the time permitted by the New Jersey Court Rules.

_____
(Defendant's signature)   Defendant, *Pro Se*

_____
(Defendant's name printed)

Name _____
       (Defendant's name, address, and telephone number)

Address _____

_____

Telephone _____

Defendant, *Pro Se*

SUPERIOR COURT OF NEW JERSEY
CHANCERY DIVISION—FAMILY PART

_____ COUNTY
       (County where divorce complaint is filed)

DOCKET NO. FM _____
                    (Docket number of divorce case)

_____

Name: _____   CIVIL ACTION
                 Plaintiff

           vs.   **ANSWER AND
                                                        COUNTERCLAIM
Name: _____   FOR DIVORCE**
                 Defendant   **Based on Extreme Cruelty**

_____

The defendant, _____, residing at
                          (Defendant's name)

_____,
                          (Defendant's address)

_____ County, State of _____, by way of answer to the

plaintiff's complaint says:

1. I _____ the allegations contained in paragraph 1.
      (Admit/deny)

2. I _____ the allegations contained in paragraph 2.
      (Admit/deny)

3. I _____ the allegations contained in paragraph 3.
      (Admit/deny)

4. I _____ the allegations contained in paragraph 4.
      (Admit/deny)

5. I _____ the allegations contained in paragraph 5.
   (Admit/deny)

6. I _____ the allegations contained in paragraph 6.
   (Admit/deny)

7. I _____ the allegations contained in paragraph 7.
   (Admit/deny)

8. I _____ the allegations contained in paragraph 8.
   (Admit/deny)

WHEREFORE, defendant demands judgment dismissing plaintiff's

complaint together with interests and costs of suit.

COUNTERCLAIM FOR DIVORCE
Based on Extreme Cruelty

1. The defendant was lawfully married to _____,
   (Plaintiff's name)

the plaintiff herein, on _____ in a _____
                          (Date of the marriage)   (Type of ceremony)

ceremony performed by _____.
                      (Name of the person who performed the ceremony)

2. The plaintiff has been guilty of extreme cruelty toward the defendant

beginning on or about _____, continuing from that
                      (Date on which plaintiff began his/her acts of extreme cruelty toward you)

day until _____. The specific acts of cruelty
          (Present date or date on which acts of cruelty stopped)

committed by plaintiff are as follows:

A. On or about _____, plaintiff
                (Date act of cruelty was committed)

   _____
   (Description of the act of extreme cruelty)

   _____

   _____.

B. On or about _____, plaintiff
                (Date act of cruelty was committed)

   _____
   (Description of the act of extreme cruelty)

   _____

   _____.

C. On or about _____, plaintiff
(Date act of cruelty was committed)

_____
(Description of the act of extreme cruelty)

_____

_____.

D. On or about _____, plaintiff
(Date act of cruelty was committed)

_____
(Description of the act of extreme cruelty)

_____

_____.

3. It has been more than three months since the last act of extreme cruelty listed above.

4. At the point at which plaintiff committed the above-noted acts of cruelty towards the defendant, defendant was a *bona fide* resident of the State of New Jersey. Since that date, and for more than one year before the date of filing this counterclaim, defendant has continued to be a *bona fide* resident of this state.

5. At the point at which plaintiff committed the most recent acts of extreme cruelty towards defendant, defendant lived at _____
(Defendant's address at the time of the most recent acts of cruelty)

_____,

City of _____, County of _____, State of New Jersey.

6. The plaintiff, _____, resides at
(Plaintiff's name)

_____
(Plaintiff's address)

_____.

7. (Check the appropriate statement below and fill in information where applicable.)

____ A. No children were born of this marriage.

____ B. The following children were born of this marriage:

_____ _____
(Name)   (Birth date)

_____   _____
(Name)   (Birth date)

_____   _____
(Name)   (Birth date)

_____   _____
(Name)   (Birth date)

____ C. An order for child support was entered on _____
                                                                                    (Date of original order)

docket number _____.
                             (Docket number of child support case)

8. The plaintiff and defendant in the matter within have been parties to the

following prior actions:

(List any other court cases where you or your spouse are involved in a lawsuit, such as cases for bankruptcy, personal injury, child support, custody, domestic violence, etc.)

A. _____   _____
                     (Caption or title of case)   (Docket number)

B. _____   _____
                     (Caption or title of case)   (Docket number)

C. _____   _____
                     (Caption or title of case)   (Docket number)

D. _____   _____
                     (Caption or title of case)   (Docket number)

WHEREFORE, defendant demands judgment:

(Check the appropriate statement below and fill in information where applicable)

____ A. Dissolving the marriage between the parties;

____ B. Ordering that all debts and assets be equitably distributed between the

parties;

____ C. Ordering that plaintiff pay child support to defendant;

____ D. Ordering that defendant have physical custody of/be the parent of

primary custody for the minor children of the marriage;

____ E. Ordering that plaintiff pay alimony to defendant;

____ F. Permitting defendant to assume the use of the name of

_____;
                  (The name that you would like to assume after your divorce)

_____ G. Granting such further relief as the Court may deem just and equitable.

_____
(Defendant's signature)   Defendant, *Pro Se*

_____
(Defendant's name printed)

Dated _____
(Date on which defendant signs this document)

CERTIFICATION OF VERIFICATION AND NON-COLLUSION PURSUANT TO R. 4:5-1

1. I am the defendant in the foregoing counterclaim.

2. The allegations of the counterclaim are true to the best of my knowledge, information, and belief. The counterclaim is made in truth and good faith and without collusion for the causes set forth therein.

3. The matter in controversy in the within action is not the subject of any other action pending in any court or of a pending arbitration proceeding, nor is any such court action or arbitration proceeding presently contemplated. There are no other persons who should be joined in this action at this time.

I certify that the foregoing statements made by me are true. I am aware that if any of the foregoing statements made by me are willfully false, I am subject to punishment.

_____
(Defendant's signature)   Defendant, *Pro Se*

_____
(Defendant's name printed)

Dated _____
(Date on which defendant signs this document)

The undersigned hereby certifies that this pleading was served within the time permitted by the New Jersey Court Rules.

_____
(Defendant's signature)   Defendant, *Pro Se*

Name _____
      (Defendant's name, address, and telephone number)

Address _____

_____

Telephone _____

Defendant, *Pro Se*

SUPERIOR COURT OF NEW JERSEY
CHANCERY DIVISION—FAMILY PART

_____ COUNTY
      (County where divorce complaint is filed)

DOCKET NO. FM _____
                    (Docket number of divorce case)

Name: _____ Plaintiff vs. Name: _____ Defendant	CIVIL ACTION **ANSWER AND COUNTERCLAIM FOR DIVORCE** **Based on Irreconcilable Differences**

The defendant, _____, residing at
                    (Defendant's name)

_____,
      (Defendant's address)

_____ County, State of _____, by way of answer to the

plaintiff's complaint says:

1. I _____ the allegations contained in paragraph 1.
     (Admit/deny)

2. I _____ the allegations contained in paragraph 2.
     (Admit/deny)

3. I _____ the allegations contained in paragraph 3.
     (Admit/deny)

4. I _____ the allegations contained in paragraph 4.
     (Admit/deny)

5. I _____ the allegations contained in paragraph 5.
   (Admit/deny)

6. I _____ the allegations contained in paragraph 6.
   (Admit/deny)

7. I _____ the allegations contained in paragraph 7.
   (Admit/deny)

8. I _____ the allegations contained in paragraph 8.
   (Admit/deny)

WHEREFORE, defendant demands judgment dismissing plaintiff's complaint together with interests and costs of suit.

COUNTERCLAIM FOR DIVORCE

Based on Irreconcilable Differences

1. The defendant was lawfully married to _____,
   (Plaintiff's name)
   the plaintiff herein, on _____ in a _____
   (Date of the marriage)   (Type of ceremony)
   ceremony performed by _____.
   (Name of the person who performed the ceremony)

2. Plaintiff and defendant have experienced irreconcilable differences for a period of six months,

3. Those irreconcilable differences have caused the breakdown of the marriage.

4. There is no reasonable prospect of reconciliation between plaintiff and defendant.

5. For more than one year before the date of filing of this complaint, defendant has continued to be a *bona fide* resident of this state.

6. At the point at which defendant and plaintiff had experienced irreconcilable differences for a period of six months, defendant lived at _____

_____,
(Defendant's address at that time)

City of _____, County of _____, and

State of _____.

7. The plaintiff, _____, resides at_____
(Plaintiff's name)

_____,
(Plaintiff's address)

8. (Check the appropriate statement below and fill in information where applicable)

____ A. No children were born of this marriage.

____ B. The following children were born of this marriage:

_____	_____
(Name)	(Birth date)
_____	_____
(Name)	(Birth date)
_____	_____
(Name)	(Birth date)
_____	_____
(Name)	(Birth date)

____C. An order for child support was entered on _____
(Date of original order)

under docket number _____.
(Docket number of child support case)

9. The plaintiff and defendant in this matter have been parties to the

following prior actions:

(List any other court cases where you or your spouse are involved in a lawsuit, such as cases for bankruptcy, personal injury, child support, custody, domestic violence, etc.)

A. _____ _____
(Caption or title of case)   (Docket number)

B. _____ _____
(Caption or title of case)   (Docket number)

C. _____ _____
(Caption or title of case)   (Docket number)

D. _____ _____
(Caption or title of case)   (Docket number

WHEREFORE, defendant demands judgment:

(Check the appropriate statement below and fill in information where applicable)

____ A. Dissolving the marriage between the parties;

____ B. Ordering that all debts and assets be equitably distributed between the parties;

____ C. Ordering that plaintiff pay child support to defendant;

____ D. Ordering that defendant have physical custody of/be the parent of primary custody for the minor children of the marriage;

____ E. Ordering that plaintiff pay alimony to defendant;

____ F. Permitting defendant to assume the use of the name of

_____;

(The name that you would like to assume after your divorce)

____ G. Granting such further relief as the Court may deem just and equitable.

_____

(Defendant's signature)

_____

(Defendant's name printed)   Defendant, *Pro Se*

Dated _____

(Date on which defendant signs this document)

CERTIFICATION OF VERIFICATION AND NON-COLLUSION PURSUANT TO R. 4:5-1

1. I am the defendant in the foregoing counterclaim.

2. The allegations of the counterclaim are true to the best of my knowledge, information, and belief. The counterclaim is made in truth and good faith and without collusion for the causes set forth therein.

3. The matter in controversy in the within action is not the subject of any other action pending in any court or of a pending arbitration proceeding, nor is any such court action or arbitration proceeding presently contemplated. There are no other persons who should be joined in this action at this time.

I certify that the foregoing statements made by me are true. I am aware that if any of the foregoing statements made by me are willfully false, I am subject to punishment.

_____
(Defendant's signature)   Defendant, *Pro Se*

_____
(Defendant's name printed)

Dated _____
(Date on which defendant signs this document)

The undersigned hereby certifies that this pleading was served within the time permitted by the New Jersey Court Rules.

_____
(Defendant's signature)   Defendant, *Pro Se*

Name _____
        (Defendant's name, address, and telephone number)

Address _____

_____

Telephone _____

Date _____

Defendant, *Pro Se*

Superior Court of New Jersey

_____ County Family Part
(County where divorce complaint is filed)

_____
        (Fill in address from Appendix A)

_____

_____, New Jersey _____
        (City)   (Zip code)

ATTENTION: FILING CLERK

     RE: _____ Docket No. FM _____
            (Caption/title of divorce case)   (Docket number of divorce case)

Dear Madam/Sir:

     Enclosed please find the following documents related to the above divorce matter:

        (Place a check next to items enclosed)

        ___ 1. Answer and counterclaim for divorce and attached certification of verification and non-collusion.
        ___ 2. Certification of insurance.
        ___ 3. Certification of notification of complementary dispute resolution.
        ___ 4. Request for waiver of fees and supporting certification.
        ___ 5. Form of order permitting waiver of fees.
        ___ 6. Check or money order for filing fee. (If fees are not waived)
        ___ 7. Family case information statement.
        ___ 8. Confidential litigant information sheet.
        ___ 9. Check or money order for Parents' Education Program fee. (If you have children)

     Kindly file the enclosed documents, retain the originals, and return two copies of each document marked "filed" in the enclosed stamped, self-addressed envelope.

                                Very truly yours,

                        _____
                                    (Your signature)

Name _____
(Plaintiff's name, address, and telephone number)

Address _____

_____

Telephone _____

Plaintiff, *Pro Se*

SUPERIOR COURT OF NEW JERSEY
CHANCERY DIVISION—FAMILY PART

_____ COUNTY
(County where divorce complaint is filed)

DOCKET NO. FM _____
(Docket number of divorce case)

Name: _____
Plaintiff

vs.

Name: _____
Defendant

CIVIL ACTION

**ANSWER TO
COUNTERCLAIM
FOR DIVORCE**

Plaintiff, _____, residing at
(Plaintiff's name)

_____
(Plaintiff's address)

_____, _____, by way of answer to

the defendant's counterclaim filed herein says:

1. I _____ the allegations contained in paragraph 1 of the counterclaim.
   (Admit/deny)

2. I _____ the allegations contained in paragraph 2 of the counterclaim.
   (Admit/deny)

3. I _____ the allegations contained in paragraph 3 of the counterclaim.
   (Admit/deny)

4. I _____ the allegations contained in paragraph 4 of the counterclaim.
   (Admit/deny)

223

5. I _____ the allegations contained in paragraph 5 of the counterclaim.
    (Admit/deny)

6. I _____ the allegations contained in paragraph 6 of the counterclaim.
    (Admit/deny)

7. I _____ the allegations contained in paragraph 7 of the counterclaim.
    (Admit/deny)

8. I _____ the allegations contained in paragraph 8 of the counterclaim.
    (Admit/deny)

Defendant-counterclaimant is estopped from obtaining a judgment of divorce

on the counterclaim based upon _____, as alleged in
(Choose separation, desertion, or extreme cruelty)

paragraph(s) _____ of the counterclaim,
(Specific paragraph(s) of the counterclaim you are objecting to)

which allegations are incorporated herein and made part of this answer to counterclaim as

though they were set forth herein.

WHEREFORE, plaintiff demands judgment dismissing defendant's

counterclaim together with counsel fees and costs.

_____
(Your signature)   Plaintiff, *Pro Se*

_____
(Your name printed)

Dated _____
(Date on which you sign this document)

Name _____
(Plaintiff's name, address, and telephone number)

Address _____

_____

Telephone _____

Date _____

Plaintiff, *Pro Se*

Superior Court of New Jersey

_____ County Family Part
(County where divorce complaint is filed)

_____
(Fill in address from Appendix A)

_____

_____, New Jersey _____
(City)   (Zip code)

ATTENTION: FILING CLERK

RE: _____ Docket No. FM _____
(Caption/title of divorce case)   (Docket number of divorce case)

Dear Madam/Sir:

Enclosed please find an original and two copies of plaintiff's answer to defendant's counterclaim for divorce in the above matter.

Kindly file the enclosed documents, retain the original, and return two copies marked "filed" in the enclosed self-addressed, stamped envelope.

Very truly yours,

_____
(Plaintiff's signature)

Name:_____
(Plaintiff's or defendant's name, address, and telephone number)

Address:_____

_____

Telephone:_____

_____, *Pro Se*
(Plaintiff or defendant)

SUPERIOR COURT OF NEW JERSEY
CHANCERY DIVISION—FAMILY PART

_____ COUNTY
(County where divorce complaint is filed)

DOCKET NO. FM _____
(Docket number of divorce case)

Name: _____

Plaintiff

vs.

Name: _____

Defendant

CIVIL ACTION

**CERTIFICATION
OF
SERVICE**

I, _____, _____ *pro se*
(Plaintiff's or defendant's name) (Plaintiff or defendant)

in the within action, hereby certify that on the date below, an original and two copies of

_____,
(List titles of documents that you are filing with the court)

were filed with the Clerk of the Superior Court, _____
(Name and address of the county court where filed)

_____.

I further certify that on _____, a
(Date documents were mailed to plaintiff/defendant)

copy of each of the above-listed documents was sent by regular and certified mail to the

_____ at the following address:
(Plaintiff or defendant, or plaintiff's or defendant's attorney)

226

_____
(Plaintiff's or defendant's, or plaintiff's or defendant's attorney's name and address)

_____

_____

_____

I hereby certify that the foregoing statements made by me are true. I am aware that if any of the foregoing statements made by me are willfully false, I am subject to punishment.

_____
(Plaintiff's or defendant's signature) Plaintiff or Defendant, *Pro Se*

_____
(Plaintiff's or defendant's name printed)

Dated _____
(Date on which document is signed)

Name _____
(Plaintiff's name, address, and telephone number)

Address _____

_____

Telephone _____

Plaintiff, *Pro Se*

SUPERIOR COURT OF NEW JERSEY
CHANCERY DIVISION—FAMILY PART

_____ COUNTY
(County where divorce complaint is filed)

DOCKET NO. FM _____
(Docket number of divorce case)

Name: _____ Plaintiff	CIVIL ACTION
vs.	**REQUEST TO ENTER DEFAULT JUDGMENT AND SUPPORTING CERTIFICATION**
Name: _____ Defendant	

To the Clerk of the above-named Court:

Please enter upon the docket the default of the defendant _____
(Defendant's name)

_____ in the above entitled action for failure to plead or

otherwise defend as provided by the Rules of Civil Practice or by an order of this Court,

or because the answer of the defendant has been stricken.

_____
(Your name)   Plaintiff, *Pro se*

1. I am the plaintiff in the above-entitled action.

2. The summons and a copy of the complaint in this action were served upon

_____ on
(Defendant's name)

_____.
(Date that defendant was served with the divorce summons and complaint)

228

3. Proof of service is supported by the following documents, which are attached as exhibits to this certification.

    (Put a check by the statement describing the applicable document)

    _____ A. The sheriff's proof of service filed with the Court, dated

    _____.
    (Date signed by sheriff's officer on proof of service/return of process form)

    _____ B. The acknowledgment of service form filed with the Court,

    dated _____.
    (Date that defendant signed acknowledgment of service form)

    _____ C. The return receipt from mailing the summons and complaint to

    the defendant, dated _____.
    (Date signed by recipient of mailed items on return receipt)

    _____ D. The order permitting substituted service, dated

    _____.
    (Date that the court signed the order)

    _____ E. The order permitting service by publication, dated

    _____.
    (Date that the court signed the order)

4. The time within which the defendant may answer or otherwise respond to the complaint has expired, has not been extended or enlarged, and the defendant has not answered or otherwise responded.

I certify that the foregoing statements made by me are true. I am aware that if any of the foregoing statements made by me are willfully false, I am subject to punishment.

_____
(Plaintiff's signature)   Plaintiff, *Pro Se*

_____
(Plaintiff's name printed)

Dated _____
(Date on which plaintiff signs this document)

Name _____
(Plaintiff's name, address, and telephone number)

Address _____

_____

Telephone _____

Date _____

Plaintiff, *Pro Se*

Superior Court of New Jersey

_____ County Family Part
(County where divorce complaint is filed)

_____
(Fill in address from Appendix A)

_____

_____, New Jersey _____
(City)   (Zip code)

ATTENTION: FILING CLERK

RE: _____ Docket No. FM _____
(Caption/title of divorce case)   (Docket number of divorce case)

Dear Madam/Sir:

Enclosed please find an original and two copies of plaintiff's request to enter default judgment and supporting certification, certification of non-military service, and certification of service in the above matter.

Kindly file the enclosed documents, retain the originals, and return two copies marked "filed" in the enclosed self-addressed, stamped envelope.

I request that, after the entry of default, the matter be listed for a default hearing.

(Choose the statement below that accurately reflects the type of relief you are seeking)

_____ I am seeking only a divorce and/or name change. Therefore, please schedule the default hearing as soon as possible.

_____ In addition to a divorce, I am seeking other relief such as child support, alimony, and/or equitable distribution, which requires that I serve upon the

defendant a notice of application for equitable distribution at least 20 days prior to the hearing date. Therefore, in order to give the defendant time to receive this notice, please schedule the default hearing with at least 40 days' notice to me.

Very truly yours,

_____
(Plaintiff's signature)

Name _____
(Plaintiff's name, address, and telephone number)

Address _____

_____

Telephone _____

Plaintiff, *Pro Se*

SUPERIOR COURT OF NEW JERSEY
CHANCERY DIVISION—FAMILY PART

_____ COUNTY
(County where divorce complaint is filed)

DOCKET NO. FM _____
(Docket number of divorce case)

Name: _____ Plaintiff vs. Name: _____ Defendant	CIVIL ACTION **CERTIFICATION OF NON-MILITARY SERVICE**

I, _____, of full age, hereby
(Plaintiff's name)

certify as follows:

1. I am the plaintiff in the above-entitled matter.

(Choose either #2 or #3 and cross out the paragraph that does not apply)

2. I am unable to determine whether the defendant is in military service at this time.

The details of how I attempted to get information about the defendant's military

status are as follows:

a. On or about _____,
(Date that you attempted to get information about the defendant)

_____
(Description of what you did)

_____

232

b. On or about _____,

(Date that you attempted to get information about the defendant)

_____

(Description of what you did)

_____

c. On or about _____,

(Date that you attempted to get information about the defendant)

_____

(Description of what you did)

_____

d. On or about _____,

(Date that you attempted to get information about the defendant)

_____

(Description of what you did)

_____

3. I know that the defendant named herein is not in the military service of the United States by way of the following information:

(Check the statement or statements that apply)

_____ Official information received from the military. (Attached hereto are Exhibits supporting this statement.)

_____ Personal knowledge and contact. The specific details of this knowledge and contact are as follows:

a. On or about _____,

(Date that you received information about or had contact with the defendant)

_____

(Description of the information or contact)

_____

b. On or about _____,

(Date that you received information about or had contact with the defendant)

_____

(Description of the information or contact)

_____

c. On or about _____,
(Date that you received information about or had contact with the defendant)

_____
(Description of the information or contact)

_____

d. On or about _____,
(Date that you received information about or had contact with the defendant)

_____
(Description of the information or contact)

_____

4. I hereby certify that the foregoing statements made by me are true. I am aware that if any of the foregoing statements made by me are willfully false I may be subject to punishment.

_____
(Plaintiff's signature)

Plaintiff, *Pro Se*

_____
(Plaintiff's name printed)

Dated _____
(Date on which plaintiff signs this document)

Name _____
        (Plaintiff's name, address, and telephone number)

Address _____

_____

Telephone _____

Plaintiff, *Pro Se*

SUPERIOR COURT OF NEW JERSEY
CHANCERY DIVISION—FAMILY PART

_____ COUNTY
        (County where divorce complaint is filed)

DOCKET NO. FM _____
                    (Docket number of divorce case)

Name: _____
                    Plaintiff

vs.

Name: _____
                    Defendant

CIVIL ACTION

**NOTICE OF DEFAULT
DIVORCE HEARING**

TO: _____
        (Name and address of defendant or defendant's attorney)

_____

_____

_____

    PLEASE TAKE NOTICE, that on _____,
                                    (Date the default divorce hearing is scheduled)
the above-referenced matter will be heard before

The Honorable _____, J.S.C.,
                (Name of the judge who will be hearing your case)

at _____, in the _____ County Superior
    (Time of appearance scheduled by the court)   (County)

Court, at _____
                    (Address of the courthouse)

_____, New Jersey.

_____
                (Plaintiff's signature)

Dated _____
        (Date on which plaintiff signs this document)

235

Name _____
(Plaintiff's name and address)

Address _____

_____

Date _____

Plaintiff, *Pro Se*

_____
(Name and address of defendant or defendant's attorney)

_____

_____

_____

RE: _____ Docket No. FM _____
(Caption/title of divorce case)   (Docket number of divorce case)

Dear _____:
(Defendant's name or his/her attorney's name)

Enclosed please find a copy of a notice of default divorce hearing in the above matter. Please note that this document directs you to appear for a hearing on

_____ at _____, at
(Date of hearing)   (Time of the hearing)

_____.
(Location of the hearing)

Very truly yours,

_____
(Plaintiff's signature)

Name _____
             (Plaintiff's name, address, and telephone number)

Address _____

_____

Telephone _____

Plaintiff, *Pro Se*

SUPERIOR COURT OF NEW JERSEY
CHANCERY DIVISION—FAMILY PART

_____ COUNTY
(County where divorce complaint is filed)

DOCKET NO. FM _____
(Docket number of divorce case)

Name: _____
          Plaintiff

         vs.

Name: _____
         Defendant

CIVIL ACTION

NOTICE OF APPLICATION FOR EQUITABLE DISTRIBUTION

TO: _____
     (Name and address of defendant or his/her attorney, if applicable)

_____

_____

_____

PLEASE TAKE NOTICE, that on _____,
                             (Date the default divorce hearing is scheduled)

the above-referenced matter will be heard before The Honorable

_____, J.S.C.,
     (Name of the judge who will be hearing your case)

at _____, in the _____ County Superior
  (Time of appearance scheduled by the court) (County where divorce complaint is filed)

Court, at _____
             (Address of the courthouse—see Appendix A)

_____, New Jersey.

PLEASE TAKE FURTHER NOTICE that plaintiff is seeking judgment:

1. Equitably distributing the property of the marriage, which is the subject of this divorce action between the named parties. The property that plaintiff requests be given to _____ includes the following:
   (Her/him)

(List and describe real or personal marital property that you are asking be given to you)

A. _____

B. _____

C. _____

D. _____

E. _____

F. _____

G. _____

H. _____

I. _____

J. _____

K. _____

PLEASE TAKE FURTHER NOTICE that plaintiff is seeking judgment

(Check the applicable statements)

_____ Compelling the defendant to pay child support for the minor child(ren) of the marriage in the amount of _____.
(List amount of child support per week that you are requesting)

_____ Compelling the defendant to pay alimony to the plaintiff in the amount of _____.
(List amount of alimony per week that you are requesting)

_____ Compelling the defendant to maintain a life insurance policy on _____
(His/her)
life naming the child(ren) as irrevocable beneficiary(ies) and plaintiff as trustee.

_____ Compelling the defendant to maintain full health insurance, including dental insurance, for the benefit of the child(ren).

_____ Compelling the defendant to be liable for future medical, dental, prescription drugs, and eyeglass expenses for the minor child(ren) that are not otherwise covered under the defendant's health insurance policy, Medicaid, or other health care program.

_____ _____

(Write in additional requests)

_____

_____

_____

_____

_____

_____

_____

_____

_____

This notice has been filed with the Superior Court, Chancery Division, Family Part, _____ County. This notice can be examined by the

(County where divorce complaint is filed)

defendant in this action during normal business hours at the Family Division Manager's Office of the Superior Court located at _____

(Address of the courthouse where divorce complaint is filed)

_____.

_____

(Plaintiff's signature)   Plaintiff, _Pro Se_

_____

(Plaintiff's name printed)

Dated _____

(Date on which plaintiff signs this document)

Name _____
(Plaintiff's name, address, and telephone number)

Address _____

_____

Telephone _____

Date _____

Plaintiff, *Pro Se*

Superior Court of New Jersey

_____ County Family Part
(County where divorce complaint is filed)

_____
(Fill in address from Appendix A)

_____

_____, New Jersey _____
(City)   (Zip code)

ATTENTION: FILING CLERK

    RE: _____ Docket No. FM _____
        (Caption/title of divorce case)   (Docket number of divorce case)

Dear Madam/Sir:

    Enclosed please find an original and two copies of plaintiff's notice of equitable distribution and certification of service in the above matter.

    Kindly file the enclosed documents, retain the originals, and return two copies marked "filed" in the enclosed self-addressed, stamped envelope.

                        Very truly yours,

                      _____
                          (Plaintiff's signature)

Name _____
(Plaintiff's name, address, and telephone number)

Address _____

_____

Telephone _____

Plaintiff, *Pro Se*

SUPERIOR COURT OF NEW JERSEY
CHANCERY DIVISION—FAMILY PART

_____ COUNTY
(County where divorce complaint is filed)

DOCKET NO. FM _____
(Docket number of divorce case)

_____

Name: _____
Plaintiff

vs.

Name: _____
Defendant

_____

CIVIL ACTION

**FINAL DEFAULT
JUDGMENT OF
DIVORCE**

THIS MATTER HAVING BEEN heard before The Honorable

_____, J.S.C.,
(Name of the judge in your divorce case)

on the _____ day of _____, 20_____,
              (Date)   (Month)   (Year)

in the presence of the plaintiff, _____,
                                                              (Plaintiff's name)

appearing *pro se*, and the defendant, _____,
                                                                (Defendant's name)

having failed to appear or answer, and it appearing that the defendant was properly

served with process and provided with all requisite notice in accordance with Court

Rules; and upon the complaint of plaintiff and the proofs presented to the Court; and the

Court having heard and considered the proofs in this action; and it appearing that plaintiff

and the defendant were married to each other on _____
                                                                                    (Date of your marriage)

in a _____ ceremony in _____;
(Type of ceremony)   (Location of the marriage ceremony)

and it appearing that plaintiff pleaded and proved a cause of action for divorce based on

_____, under the relevant statute,
(Choose 18-month separation, or desertion, or extreme cruelty, or irreconcilable differences)

N.J.S.A. 2A:34-2 *et seq.*; and it appearing that at the time the cause of action for divorce

arose, the plaintiff was a *bona fide* resident of this state, and that plaintiff has been a *bona*

fide resident of this state, for one year since filing this action; and it further appearing that

jurisdiction has been acquired over both parties, and for good cause shown,

IT IS, on this _____ day of _____, 20_____,
(DO NOT WRITE HERE)

ORDERED AND ADJUDGED, by virtue of the power and authority of this

Court, that the plaintiff, _____, and the
(Plaintiff's name)

defendant, _____, be divorced from the
(Defendant's name)

bonds of matrimony and that each of them be freed and discharged from the obligation

thereof; and

IT IS FURTHER ORDERED THAT:

1. (Check the appropriate statement and fill in the appropriate information)

____ A. The _____ shall have primary physical custody of
            (Plaintiff or defendant)

the minor children of the marriage.

____ B. The plaintiff and defendant shall have joint physical custody of

the minor children of the marriage.

(Fill in the name[s] and birth date[s] of the minor child[ren] of the marriage)

_____	_____
(Child's name)	(Child's birth date)
_____	_____
(Child's name)	(Child's birth date)
_____	_____
(Child's name)	(Child's birth date)
_____	_____
(Child's name)	(Child's birth date)
_____	_____
(Child's name)	(Child's birth date)

2. (Check the appropriate statement and fill in the appropriate information)

_____ A. The _____ shall have primary legal custody of the
          (Plaintiff or defendant)

   minor children and shall be responsible for making major decisions

   concerning the health, education, and general welfare of the children.

_____ B. The plaintiff and defendant shall have joint legal custody of the

   minor children and shall consult with each other about major decisions

   concerning the health, education, and general welfare of the children.

3. The _____ shall be awarded the following
                  (Plaintiff or defendant)

   visitation/parenting time with the minor children:

   (List the days, times, and details of visits, including drop-off and pick-up of the children and holiday
   visitation)

   _____

   _____

   _____

   _____

   _____

   _____

4. The _____ shall pay to the _____
              (Plaintiff or defendant)   (Plaintiff or defendant)

   _____ per week for child support. Payments shall be made
   (Amount of weekly child support)

   via wage garnishment.

5. Prior to the onset of the wage garnishment, the _____
                                                            (Plaintiff or defendant)

   shall make payments directly to:

   (Check the appropriate statement)

   _____ A. The probation department of the County of

       _____.
                (County where plaintiff or defendant lives)

   _____ B. Directly to the _____.
                                (Plaintiff or defendant)

6. The _____ shall contribute to the future cost of college
   (Plaintiff or defendant)

   education or vocational education for the minor _____
   (Child or children)

   of the marriage until such time as the minor _____
   (Child or children)

   graduate(s) or complete(s) the chosen course of college or vocational study.

7. The _____ shall maintain medical insurance
   (Plaintiff or defendant)

   for the benefit of the minor _____ of the marriage.
   (Child or children)

8. The _____ shall be liable for ___ percent of any
   (Plaintiff or defendant)

   future medical, dental, prescription drug, and eyeglass expenses necessary for

   the minor _____ of the marriage that are not otherwise
   (Child or children)

   covered under the _____ health insurance policy,
   (Plaintiff's or defendant's)

   Medicaid, or other health care program.

9. The _____ shall maintain a life insurance policy
   (Plaintiff or defendant)

   on _____ life for the exclusive benefit of the _____
   (His or her)   (Child or children)

   and naming the _____ as beneficiary and the
   (Child or children)

   _____ as trustee.
   (Plaintiff or defendant)

10. The _____ shall pay to the _____
    (Plaintiff or defendant)   (Plaintiff or defendant)

    $_____ per week as alimony. Payments shall be made for
    (Amount of weekly alimony)

    _____ years or until such time as plaintiff remarries.
    (Number of years of alimony)

    Payments shall be made via wage garnishment.

11. Prior to the onset of the wage garnishment, _____ shall
    (Plaintiff or defendant)

    make payments directly to:

    (Check the appropriate statement.)

    ____ A. The probation department of the County of _____
    (County where plaintiff or defendant lives)

    ____ B. Directly to the _____
    (Plaintiff or defendant)

12. The plaintiff shall resume the use of this name:

_____.
(Name that plaintiff would like to assume after divorce)

13. The following prior orders concerning other matters between the parties

shall remain in full force and effect and are hereby incorporated into this final

judgment of divorce.

(If applicable, fill in the appropriate statement[s] below)

A. The domestic violence final restraining order dated

_____, issued by the
(Date that the court signed the order)

_____ County Superior Court, Docket
(County where the order was issued)

Number _____ shall remain in effect.

B. The visitation order dated _____, issued
(Date that the court signed the order)

by the _____ County Superior Court, Docket
(County where the order was issued)

Number _____, shall remain in effect.

C. The support order dated _____, issued by the
(Date that the court signed the order)

_____ County Superior Court, Docket
(County where the order was issued)

Number _____, shall remain in effect.

The Honorable _____, J.S.C.
(DO NOT WRITE HERE)

Name _____
(Plaintiff's name and address)

Address _____

_____

Date _____

VIA CERTIFIED AND REGULAR MAIL

_____
(Name and address of your spouse or your spouse's attorney)

_____

_____

_____

RE: _____ Docket No. FM _____
(Caption/title of divorce case)   (Docket number of divorce case)

Dear _____:
(Name of your spouse or your spouse's attorney)

Enclosed please find a copy of a final default judgment of divorce in the above matter, which has been filed with the court.

_____
(Plaintiff's signature)

Name _____
(Plaintiff's or defendant's name, address, and telephone number)

Address _____

_____

Telephone _____

_____, *Pro Se*
(Plaintiff or defendant)

SUPERIOR COURT OF NEW JERSEY
CHANCERY DIVISION—FAMILY PART

_____ COUNTY
(County where divorce complaint is filed)

DOCKET NO. FM _____
(Docket number of divorce case)

Name: _____
Plaintiff

vs.

Name: _____
Defendant

CIVIL ACTION

**CUSTODY AND
PARENTING TIME/
VISITATION PLAN**
Pursuant to R. 5:8-5

I am the _____ in the above action. I submit this parenting
(Plaintiff or defendant)

plan in accordance with Rule 5:8-5.

1. Plaintiff resides at _____
   (Plaintiff's address)

   _____

2. Defendant resides at _____
   (Defendant's address)

   _____

3. Plaintiff is employed as _____
   (Plaintiff's job title)

   at _____
   (Name and address of plaintiff's employer)

   _____

   _____.

4. Defendant is employed as _____
   (Defendant's job title)

   at _____
   (Name and address of defendant's employer)

   _____

   _____.

5. _____ requests the following:
   (Plaintiff or defendant)

   (Check the applicable statement)

   ____ A. _____ shall be the parent of primary residence and
   (Plaintiff or defendant)

   _____ shall have visitation/parenting time.
   (Plaintiff or defendant)

   ____ B. Plaintiff and defendant shall share joint physical/residential custody

   of the minor child(ren).

   ____ C. Plaintiff and defendant shall share joint legal custody of the

   minor child(ren).

   ____ D. _____ shall have primary legal and physical
   (Plaintiff or defendant)

   custody of the minor child(ren).

   ____ E. _____ shall not have physical or legal
   (Plaintiff or defendant)

   custody of the minor child(ren) and shall have only visitation/parenting time.

   ____ F. _____
   (Other request pertaining to custody or visitation/parenting time)

   _____

   _____.

6. _____ requests the following:
   (Plaintiff or defendant)

   (Check the applicable statements)

   ____ A. _____ shall have parenting time with the
   (Plaintiff or defendant)

   child(ren) every other weekend from _____ on _____
   (Time of day)   (Day of the week)

   until _____ on _____. The _____
   (Time of day)   (Day of the week)   (Plaintiff or defendant)

shall be responsible for picking the child(ren) up at _____

_____.
(Home of plaintiff, defendant, or other location)

____ B. _____ shall also have visitation with the child(ren)
(Plaintiff or defendant)

every week on _____ from _____
(Day of the week)   (Start time)

until _____. The _____ shall be responsible
(End time)   (Plaintiff or defendant)

for dropping the child(ren) off at _____
(Home of plaintiff, defendant, or other location)

_____.

____ C. _____ shall visit with the child(ren) on
(Plaintiff or defendant)

alternate holidays beginning with _____
(Name and date of holiday that visitation schedule begins)

_____, 20_____. For the purposes of this

parenting time/visitation plan, the following is a list of holidays to be

celebrated by plaintiff or defendant and child(ren):

(List the holidays that plaintiff, defendant, and family celebrate)

_____

_____

_____

_____

_____

_____

_____

____ D. _____ shall have the child(ren) for summer
(Plaintiff or defendant)

vacation for _____ each summer. This vacation shall be
(Number of days or weeks)

scheduled at the convenience of the children, taking into consideration

school and extracurricular activity schedules.

7. Access to medical records and school records

(Check the applicable statement)

_____ A. Both the plaintiff and defendant shall have access to the

child(ren)'s school records.

_____ B. Only the _____ shall have access to the
        (Plaintiff or defendant)

child(ren)'s school records.

_____ C. Both the plaintiff and the defendant shall have access to the

child(ren)'s medical records.

_____ D. Only the _____ shall have access to the
        (Plaintiff or defendant)

child(ren)'s medical records.

_____ E. The child(ren)'s physician shall contact either the plaintiff or

the defendant to obtain consent necessary for any medical treatment, or

procedures, or testing.

_____ F. The child(ren)'s physician shall contact only the

_____ to obtain consent necessary for any medical
(Plaintiff or defendant)

treatment, or procedures, or testing.

8. Additional information

(Check the applicable statement)

_____ A. _____ is planning to move to
        (Plaintiff or defendant)

_____
(Location to which you are relocating)

on or about _____.
            (Date of proposed move)

(Explain what impact this will have on the child[ren])

_____

_____

_____

_____

_____

____ B. _____ will be changing jobs on or about
(Plaintiff or defendant)

_____
(Date of proposed move)

(Explain what impact this will have on the child[ren])

_____

_____

_____

_____

_____

I certify that the foregoing statements made by me are true. I am aware that if any of the foregoing statements made by me are willfully false, I am subject to punishment.

_____
(Plaintiff's or defendant's signature) Plaintiff or Defendant, _Pro Se_

_____
(Plaintiff's or defendant's name printed)

Dated _____
(Date on which this document is signed)

Name _____
        (Plaintiff's or defendant's name, address, and telephone number)

Address _____

_____

Telephone _____

Date _____

Plaintiff, *Pro Se*

Superior Court of New Jersey

_____ County, Family Part
        (County where divorce complaint is filed)

_____
        (Fill in address from Appendix A)

_____

_____, New Jersey _____
                (City)   (Zip code)

ATTENTION: FILING CLERK

        RE: _____ Docket No. FM _____
                (Caption/title of divorce case)   (Docket number of divorce case)

Dear Madam/Sir:

        Enclosed please find an original and two copies of _____
                                                            (Plaintiff's or defendant's)

custody and parenting time/visitation plan in the above matter.

        Kindly file the enclosed documents, retain the original, and return

two copies marked "filed" in the enclosed self-addressed, stamped envelope.

                                Very truly yours,

                                _____
                                        (Plaintiff's or defendant's signature)

Name _____
(Plaintiff's or defendant's name, address, and telephone number)

Address _____

_____

Telephone _____

_____, *Pro Se*
(Plaintiff or defendant)

SUPERIOR COURT OF NEW JERSEY
CHANCERY DIVISION—FAMILY PART
_____ COUNTY
(County where divorce complaint is filed)

DOCKET NO. FM _____
(Docket number of divorce complaint)

Name: _____
Plaintiff

vs.

Name: _____
Defendant

CIVIL ACTION

SUBPOENA DUCES TECUM ad TESTIFICANDUM

The State of New Jersey, to: _____
(Name and address of witness being commanded to appear)

_____

_____

_____

YOU ARE HEREBY COMMANDED to attend and give testimony before the

above-named Court at the _____ County Courthouse, Chancery
(County where the divorce complaint is filed)

Division, Family Part, _____
(Address of the courthouse where the trial will be held)

_____

beginning on the _____ day of _____, 20____ at 9:00 A.M.
(Beginning date of the trial)

and continuing until the close of the trial, including, if necessary, any and all additional

days beyond the beginning date, before the Honorable _____
(Name of the judge who will hear your divorce case)

on the behalf of plaintiff in the above-entitled action. You are further commanded to

bring with you and produce at the same time and place any and all records, including

photographs, related to the above matter.

    Failure to appear according to the command of this subpoena will subject you to a

penalty, damages in a civil suit, and punishment for contempt of Court.

_____, Plaintiff, *Pro Se*
(Plaintiff's signature)

_____, Plaintiff, *Pro Se*
(Plaintiff's name printed)

(Below, sign the name "Theodore J. Fetter" and initial the signature with your initials)

_____
Theodore J. Fetter
Acting Clerk, Superior Court

PROOF OF SERVICE

On _____, I, the undersigned, being
(Date you served the witness with the subpoena)

over the age of 18, served the within subpoena by:

(Check the applicable statement)

_____ 1. Mailing a copy thereof to _____
(Name of witness)

at _____
(Mailing address of witness)

_____

_____ 2. Hand delivering a copy thereof to _____
(Name of witness)

at _____
(Address at which you served witness)

_____

Address for Service

_____
(Address of witness)

_____

_____

_____

Name _____
(Plaintiff's or defendant's name and address)

Address _____

_____

_____

Date _____

VIA CERTIFIED AND REGULAR MAIL

RE: _____ Docket No. FM _____
(Caption/title of divorce case)   (Docket number of divorce case)

_____
(Name and address of witness you wish to have testify on your behalf)

_____

_____

Dear _____:
(Name of witness)

    Enclosed is a copy of a subpoena directing you to appear and give testimony in

the above-captioned matter on behalf of the _____,
(Plaintiff or defendant)

_____, at the hearing in this matter
(Plaintiff's or defendant's name)

scheduled for _____,
(Date of the hearing)

at the _____ Superior Court, at _____
(County)   (Address of the courthouse—see Appendix A)

_____.

Please contact the undersigned at your earliest convenience, prior to the hearing.

Very truly yours,

_____
(Plaintiff's or defendant's signature)

Name _____
(Plaintiff's or defendant's name, address, and telephone number)

Address _____

_____

Telephone _____

_____, *Pro Se*
(Plaintiff or defendant)

SUPERIOR COURT OF NEW JERSEY
CHANCERY DIVISION—FAMILY PART

_____ COUNTY
(County where divorce complaint is filed)

DOCKET NO. FM _____
(Docket number of divorce case)

Name: _____
Plaintiff

vs.

Name: _____
Defendant

CIVIL ACTION

**CONSENT ORDER
FINAL JUDGMENT
OF DIVORCE**

THIS MATTER HAVING BEEN heard before the Honorable

_____, J.S.C., on the
(Name of the Judge in your divorce case)

_____ day of _____, 20_____
(Day and date the divorce case was heard)

in the presence of the plaintiff, _____, appearing
(Plaintiff's name)

pro se, and the defendant _____, appearing *pro se*;
(Defendant's name)

and upon the complaint of plaintiff and the proofs presented to the Court; and the Court

having been satisfied that the defendant was served and having heard and considered the

proofs in this action; and it appearing that plaintiff and the defendant were married on

_____ in a _____ ceremony in
(Date of your marriage)   (Type of ceremony)

_____; and it appearing

that plaintiff pleaded and proved a cause of action of divorce based on

_____ under the relevant

statute, _N.J.S.A._ 2A:34-2 _et seq._; and it appearing that at the time the cause of action for

divorce arose, the plaintiff was a _bona fide_ resident of this state; and that plaintiff has

been for the one year next preceding the commencement of this action a _bona fide_

resident of this state; and it further appearing that jurisdiction has been acquired upon

both parties, and for good cause shown,

IT IS, on this _____ day of _____, 20_____,

ORDERED AND ADJUDGED, by virtue of the power and authority of the Court,

that the plaintiff, _____ and the defendant,

_____, be divorced from the bonds of matrimony

and that each of them be freed and discharged from the obligation thereof; and

IT IS FURTHER ORDERED THAT:

1. (Check the appropriate statement and fill in the appropriate information)

____ A. The _____ shall have primary physical custody of

minor children of the marriage.

____ B. The plaintiff and defendant shall have joint physical custody of

the minor children of the marriage.

(Fill in the name[s] and birth date[s] of the minor child[ren] of the marriage)

_____	_____
(Child's name)	(Child's birth date)
_____	_____
(Child's name)	(Child's birth date)
_____	_____
(Child's name)	(Child's birth date)
_____	_____
(Child's name)	(Child's birth date)
_____	_____
(Child's name)	(Child's birth date)

2. (Check the appropriate statement and fill in the appropriate information)

    ____ A. The plaintiff and defendant shall have joint legal custody of the

minor children of the marriage and shall consult with each other about

major decisions concerning the health, education, and general welfare

of the children.

    ____ B. The _____ shall have primary legal custody of
                  (Plaintiff or defendant)

the minor children and shall be responsible for making major decisions

concerning the health, education, and general welfare of the children.

3. The _____ shall be awarded the following visitation
        (Plaintiff or defendant)

with the minor children:

(List the days, times, and details of drop-off and pick-up of the children, as well as holiday
  visitations)

_____

_____

_____

_____

_____

_____

4. The _____ shall pay to the _____
       (Plaintiff or defendant)   (Plaintiff or defendant)

$_____ per week for child support. Payments shall
(Amount of weekly child support payment)

be made via wage garnishment.

5. The _____ shall pay to the _____
       (Plaintiff or defendant)   (Plaintiff or defendant)

$_____ per week for arrears (child support already owed).
(Amount of weekly child support arrears payment)

Payments shall be made via wage garnishment.

6. Prior to the onset of the wage garnishment, the _____

   (Plaintiff or defendant)

   shall make payments directly to:

   (Check the appropriate statement)

   ____ A. The probation department of the County of _____.

   (County where plaintiff/defendant lives)

   ____ B. Directly to the _____.

   (Plaintiff or defendant)

7. The_____ shall contribute to the future cost of

   (Plaintiff or defendant)

   college education or vocational education for the minor _____

   (Child/children)

   of the marriage until such time as the minor _____ graduate or

   (Child/children)

   complete the chosen course of college or vocational study.

8. The _____ shall maintain medical and health insurance

   (Plaintiff or defendant)

   for the benefit of the minor _____ of the marriage.

   (Child/children)

9. The _____ shall be liable for _____ percent of any

   (Plaintiff or defendant)

   future medical, dental, prescription drug, and eyeglass expenses necessary

   for the minor _____ of the marriage that are not otherwise

   (Child/children)

   covered under the _____ health insurance policy,

   (Plaintiff's or defendant's)

   Medicaid, or other health care program.

10. The _____ shall maintain a life insurance policy on

    (Plaintiff or defendant)

    _____ life for the exclusive benefit of the _____ and

    (His or her)   (Child/children)

    naming the _____ as beneficiary and the _____

    (Child/children)   (Plaintiff or defendant)

    as trustee.

11. The _____ shall pay to the _____

    (Plaintiff or defendant)   (Plaintiff or defendant)

    $_____ per week as alimony. Payments shall be made for

    (Weekly alimony amount)

    _____ years or until such time as plaintiff remarries.

    (Number of years of alimony)

    Payments shall be made via wage garnishment.

12. Prior to the onset of the wage garnishment, _____ shall
    (Plaintiff or defendant)

    make payments directly to:

    (Check the appropriate statement)

    ____ A. The probation department of the County of _____.
    (County where plaintiff/defendant lives)

    ____ B. Directly to the _____.
    (Plaintiff or defendant)

13. The property and debt of the marriage shall be divided between the parties

    pursuant to the settlement agreement attached hereto dated

    _____.
    (Date that property settlement agreement was signed by both parties)

14. The _____ shall assume the use of this name:
    (Plaintiff or defendant)

    _____.
    (Name that plaintiff/defendant would like to assume after the divorce)

15. The following prior orders concerning other matters between the parties shall

    remain in full force and effect and are hereby incorporated into this final

    judgment of divorce.

    (Check the appropriate statement if you have any court orders in effect)

    ____ A. The domestic violence final restraining order dated

    _____, issued by the
    (Date of the court order)

    _____ County Superior Court, Docket
    (County where order was issued)

    Number _____ shall remain
    (Docket number of the court order)

    in effect.

    ____ B. The visitation order dated _____,
    (Date of the court order)

    issued by the _____ County Superior
    (County where order was issued)

    Court, Docket Number _____, shall
    (Docket number of the court order)

    remain in effect.

_____ C. The support order dated _____,

(Date of the court order)

issued by the _____ County Superior

(County where order was issued)

Court, Docket Number _____ shall

(Docket number of the court order)

remain in effect.

The parties, having had the opportunity to review the contents of the above order,

do hereby agree to the entry of this order.

_____
(Plaintiff's signature)

_____
(Defendant's signature)

_____
(Plaintiff's name printed)   Plaintiff, _Pro Se_

_____
(Defendant's name printed)   Defendant

_____
(Date signed)

_____
(Date signed)

_____, J.S.C.

(DO NOT WRITE HERE)

Name _____
(Plaintiff's name, address, and telephone number)

Address _____

_____

Telephone _____

Plaintiff, *Pro Se*

SUPERIOR COURT OF NEW JERSEY
CHANCERY DIVISION—FAMILY PART

_____ COUNTY
(County where divorce complaint is filed)

DOCKET NO. FM _____
(Docket number of divorce case)

_____

Name: _____
          Plaintiff

          vs.

Name: _____
          Defendant

_____

CIVIL ACTION

**FINAL JUDGMENT
OF DIVORCE**

THIS MATTER HAVING BEEN heard before

The Honorable _____, J.S.C., on the
(Name of the judge in your divorce case)

_____ day of _____, 20_____,
(Day and date the divorce case was heard)

in the presence of the plaintiff, _____, appearing
(Plaintiff's name)

pro se, and the defendant, _____, appearing *pro se*;
(Defendant's name)

and upon the complaint of plaintiff and the proofs presented to the Court; and the Court

having been satisfied that the defendant was served and having heard and considered the

proofs in this action; and it appearing that plaintiff and the defendant were married on

_____ in a _____ ceremony in
(Date of your marriage)   (Type of ceremony)

_____; and it appearing
(Location of your marriage)

that plaintiff pleaded and proved a cause of action of divorce based on

_____ under the relevant
(Choose separation, or desertion, or extreme cruelty, or irreconcilable differences)

statute, *N.J.S.A.* 2A:34-2 *et seq.*; and it appearing that at the time the cause of action for

divorce arose, the plaintiff was a *bona fide* resident of this state; and that plaintiff has

been for the one year next preceding the commencement of this action a *bona fide*

resident of this state; and it further appearing that jurisdiction has been acquired upon

both parties, and for good cause shown,

IT IS, on this _____ day of _____, 20_____,
(DO NOT WRITE HERE)

ORDERED AND ADJUDGED, by virtue of the power and authority of the Court,

that the plaintiff, _____ and the defendant,
(Plaintiff's name)

_____, be divorced from the bonds of matrimony
(Defendant's name)

and that each of them be freed and discharged from the obligation thereof; and

IT IS FURTHER ORDERED THAT:

1. (Check the appropriate statement and fill in the appropriate information)

____ A. The _____ shall have primary physical custody of
(Plaintiff or defendant)

the minor children of the marriage.

____ B. The plaintiff and defendant shall have joint physical custody of

the minor children of the marriage.

(Fill in the name[s] and birth date[s] of the minor child[ren] of the marriage)

_____	_____
(Child's name)	(Child's birth date)
_____	_____
(Child's name)	(Child's birth date)
_____	_____
(Child's name)	(Child's birth date)
_____	_____
(Child's name)	(Child's birth date)
_____	_____
(Child's name)	(Child's birth date)

2. (Check the appropriate statement and fill in the appropriate information)

    ____ A. The plaintiff and defendant shall have joint legal custody of the

          minor children of the marriage and shall consult with each other about

          major decisions concerning the health, education, and general welfare

          of the children.

    ____ B. The _____ shall have primary legal custody of
                   (Plaintiff or defendant)

          the minor children and shall be responsible for making major decisions

          concerning the health, education, and general welfare of the children.

3. The _____ shall be awarded the following visitation
           (Plaintiff or defendant)

   with the minor children:

(List the days, times, and details of drop-off and pick-up of the children, as well as holiday visitations)

_____

_____

_____

_____

_____

_____

4. The _____ shall pay to the _____
          (Plaintiff or defendant)   (Plaintiff or defendant)

   $_____ per week for child support. Payments shall
   (Amount of weekly child support payment)

   be made via wage garnishment.

5. The _____ shall pay to the _____
          (Plaintiff or defendant)   (Plaintiff or defendant)

   $_____ per week for arrears (child support already owed).
   (Amount of weekly child support arrears payment)

   Payments shall be made via wage garnishment.

6. Prior to the onset of the wage garnishment, the _____
   (Plaintiff or defendant)

   shall make payments directly to:

   (Check the appropriate statement)

   ____ A. The probation department of the County of _____.
   (County where plaintiff/defendant lives)

   ____ B. Directly to the _____.
   (Plaintiff or defendant)

7. The _____ shall contribute to the future cost of
   (Plaintiff or defendant)

   college education or vocational education for the minor _____
   (Child/children)

   of the marriage until such time as the minor _____ graduate or
   (Child/children)

   complete the chosen course of college or vocational study.

8. The _____ shall maintain medical and health insurance
   (Plaintiff or defendant)

   for the benefit of the minor _____ of the marriage.
   (Child/children)

9. The _____ shall be liable for _____ percent of any
   (Plaintiff or defendant)

   future medical, dental, prescription drug, and eyeglass expenses necessary

   for the minor _____ of the marriage that are not otherwise
   (Child/children)

   covered under the _____ health insurance policy,
   (Plaintiff's or defendant's)

   Medicaid, or other health care program.

10. The _____ shall maintain a life insurance policy on
    (Plaintiff or defendant)

    _____ life for the exclusive benefit of the _____ and
    (His or her)   (Child/children)

    naming the _____ as beneficiary and the _____
    (Child/children)   (Plaintiff or defendant)

    as trustee.

11. The _____ shall pay to the _____
    (Plaintiff or defendant)   (Plaintiff or defendant)

    $_____ per week as alimony. Payments shall be made for
    (Weekly alimony amount)

    _____ years or until such time as plaintiff remarries.
    (Number of years of alimony)

    Payments shall be made via wage garnishment.

12. Prior to the onset of the wage garnishment, _____ shall
    Plaintiff or defendant)

    make payments directly to:

    (Check the appropriate statement.)

    ____ A. The probation department of the County of _____.
    (County where plaintiff/defendant lives)

    ____ B. Directly to the _____.
    (Plaintiff or defendant)

13. The property and debt of the marriage shall be divided between the parties

    pursuant to the settlement agreement attached hereto dated

    _____.
    (Date that property settlement agreement was signed by both parties)

14. The _____ shall assume the use of this name:
    (Plaintiff or defendant)

    _____.
    (Name that plaintiff/defendant would like to assume after the divorce)

15. The following prior orders concerning other matters between the parties shall

    remain in full force and effect and are hereby incorporated into this final

    judgment of divorce.

    (Check the appropriate statement if you have any court orders in effect)

    ____ A. The domestic violence final restraining order dated

    _____, issued by the
    (Date of the court order)

    _____ County Superior Court, Docket
    (County where order was issued)

    Number _____ shall remain
    (Docket number of the domestic violence final restraining order)

    in effect.

    ____ B. The visitation order dated _____,
    (Date of the court order)

    issued by the _____ County Superior
    (County where order was issued)

    Court, Docket Number _____, shall
    (Docket number of the court order)

    remain in effect.

_____ C. The support order dated _____,
(Date of the court order)

issued by the _____ County Superior
(County where order was issued)

Court, Docket Number _____ shall
(Docket number of the court order)

remain in effect.

_____, J.S.C.
(DO NOT WRITE HERE)

Name _____
(Plaintiff's or defendant's name and address)

Address _____

_____

_____

Date _____

_____
(Name and address of the judge who heard your divorce case)

_____

_____

_____

_____

      RE: _____ Docket No. FM _____
      (Caption/title of your divorce case)   (Docket number of divorce case)

Dear Judge_____:

      Pursuant to the direction of the Court, enclosed please find an original and two copies of a judgment of divorce in this matter. A copy of this order has been provided to _____ pursuant to R. 4:42-1(c) (the "five-day
(Plaintiff or defendant or plaintiff's or defendant's attorney)
rule"). If no objections to the enclosed form of order are received by the Court within five days after receipt of this correspondence, please execute the order and have a member of your staff return a copy marked "filed" in the enclosed self-addressed, stamped envelope.

      Thank you in advance for your attention to this matter.

_____
(Plaintiff's or defendant's signature) Plaintiff or Defendant, *Pro Se*

Name _____
       (Plaintiff's or defendant's name and address)

Address _____

_____

_____

Date _____

VIA CERTIFIED AND REGULAR MAIL

_____
(Plaintiff's or defendant's or plaintiff's or defendant's attorney's name and address)

_____

_____

_____

_____

          RE: _____ Docket No. FM _____
                (Caption/title of divorce case)   (Docket number of divorce case)

Dear _____:
(Plaintiff's or defendant's or plaintiff's or defendant's attorney's name)

          Enclosed please find a copy of a final judgment of divorce in this matter, stamped "filed."

                          Very truly yours,

                          _____
                                (Plaintiff's or defendant's signature)